Sturge '93

BY THE CAMBRIDGE SPRINGS HERITAGE SOCIETY

"THE RIVERSIDE INN"

In 1860, the quiet town was then called Cambridgeboro,
When Doc John Gray walked the banks, which bordered old French Creek.
He sank a probing rod into the earth hoping for black gold,
Crystal spring water spurt forth, instead of the oil he did seek.

Gray tapped this water in the valley's soil, with his old penstock
Doc excitedly thought he'd discovered oil to bring him wealth.
Instead, however, this water flowed freely for fifteen years.
Those who drank from that penstock, usually possessed good health.

His prospecting revealed four more jets of that "charged" spring water,
Which he used for treatment, or various a case and complaint.
He erected a spring house, and sold his mineral water.
Healing powers at nominal price, for the sick and for the faint.

In 1887, the charming Riverside Inn was opened.
French Creek Valley, now "Fountain Valley", began its magical lure.
The beautiful, peaceful, majestic Inn had brochures which did tell,
Of how the waters, unassisted, affected many a cure.

Franklin's Rider and Company at first, and later William Baird,
Combined the therapy of the springs, with the comforts of the Inn.
This water was sold in bottles, and fresh spring water filled the baths,
Thus, the first health spa, the Riverside Hotel just may have been.

The mineral springs brought so many changes, with their therapy.
This "Boom" prompted more than forty hotels, in this resort renown.
It brought the once calm community growing popularity,
So in 1897, Cambridge Springs, was named the town.

Passenger trains transported visitors, from far away places,
Those on board sometimes included, a United States President
Beautiful horse drawn carriages, also brought guests to the Inn,
Strolling the boardwalk to the spring house, these ladies and these gents.

Chats over games of skittle, checkers, chess, in the cozy lobby,
Ample shade of long verandas, provided for relaxation.
Dancing at the Casino Ballroom, enjoying shows on its stage,
Dining in the lovely Concord Room, fireside conversation.

Only the Riverside Inn remains, in active operation,
Of the forty hotels and many rooming houses of the past.
Enrolled in the National Register of Historic Places,
A proud history, promising future, reputation to last.

So much for the glorious past, which was once upon a time,
The tracks no longer bring passengers, and but a few freight trains.
The town bustles no more, but is still so warm and friendly,
Here at Number One, Fountain House, Fountain Street,
Riverside's charm still remains.

Weddings and receptions there, reminiscent of its origin,
As always, there's tennis and swimming, shuffleboard, a putting green.
Also featured are parties, meetings, craft fairs and dinner theaters,
Superb golf, Saturday Buffets, Sunday Bunch, like none ever seen.

Riverside - The Inn at Cambridge Springs, with class, doth still reign,
Its home, off Route 19, Crawford County, Northwestern, PA.
Visitors arrive now in bus, not buggy or train,
To step up on its porch, and return to the past so they say.

- Ronald Paul Sturga, 1993

Printed in the United States of America.

ISBN 978-0-692-99333-0

First Printing: 2017

Written by:

Dale H. Docter

Janet Beanland

Melissa Cornwell

Rose Smith

Sharon Smith Crisman

Victoria Hendrickson

Designed by:

Jesse Cornwell

CONTENTS

ACKNOWLEDGMENTS

This book is not the result of only one person's research and writing. The Cambridge Springs Heritage Society and Historical Museum has been operating since 1976 as an organization and 1995 as a museum. Much collecting and researching has been going on since then. The work of Ed Ledrick, Mary Cousins, Yetive Pulling, and more set the wheels in motion for our ability to put together this book. Today it is the continuing research of Rose Smith, Janet Beanland, Victoria Hendrickson, Sharon Smith Crisman, Melissa Cornwell, and Dale H. Docter that has allowed us to assemble the information and photographs necessary to present this history of the Riverside Inn from inception to demise, and hoped rebirth. Going above and beyond the rest, Victoria Hendrickson pursued connections in order to reach the family of Col. Parke, owner and hotel manager after the Bairds sold. The Parke descendants, Elizabeth Susan Parke Brown and Janet Cook Derrington, have generously provided a wealth of family materials that offer a new, previously obscure view of Col. Parke's years with the Riverside. Individuals from the community and beyond have come forward to share their pictures of the Riverside as well. From the time when consensus was reached to put together this book, the Heritage Society members met twice monthly to provide progress checks and a chance to see what could be done to support what the others were researching and writing. In the last chapter, a few individuals were chosen to share their memories of the Riverside. So many of us have unlimited personal memories of our experiences at the old hotel. A book could have been written just about those. We wanted to give a good cross-section of the types of memories that were made there. Thank you to all who shared with us. Equally priceless has been the knowledge and publishing skills of Melissa and Jesse Cornwell. Their skills have helped carry this project to what you have in your hands. We can't bring back our Riverside Inn, but we hope our book will in some way carry the memory forward to future generations.

- Dale H. Docter
Heritage Society President

INTRODUCTION

Mineral waters, during their heyday from the 1880s to about 1920, were said to cure all sorts of ailments. The waters also gave rise to Cambridgeboro from a sleepy little train stop town along the Atlantic & Great Western Railroad in 1884 to a community of fifteen mineral springs, twelve hotels, and in excess of forty guest cottages as well as a new name in 1897: Cambridge Springs. With Dr. John Gray's discovery of a free-flowing spring in 1859 and its mineral analysis in 1884, Dr. Gray capitalized on his find and began prescribing his waters. In the next two years the need became apparent for a sanitarium for patients arriving for Dr. Gray's mineral treatments. The Riverside Sanitarium, built on the banks of French Creek on property owned by Dr. Gray, became the first establishment to offer facilities for those seeking the mineral waters. When the sanitarium failed in 1890, this began its transformation into a hotel which offered not only mineral waters but also a fine destination for the wealthy looking to escape the heat of the cities in the summers.

Through its various owners, the Riverside survived frequent river floods, a 1909 tornado, a shift in medical practices away from mineral waters being a cure-all, the Depression, years of decline, a few years of use as a college dormitory, and even a residency of a religion-based group. Its rebirth began in 1985 with new owners Mike and Marie Halliday. In the years that followed, the grand hotel was taken back to its Victorian roots. A dinner theater was wisely added, and the hotel was redecorated using period antiques embracing its history.

What the hotel couldn't survive was fire. The hotel was laid to ruin during the early morning hours of May 2, 2017, only three weeks into its season. During its 130 years of operation, the Riverside Inn remained a constant in the community hosting untold numbers of events, celebrations, and guests. That all changed in an instant.

Using the historic photographs and archives of the Cambridge Springs Heritage Society and others, this text seeks to share the long and colorful history of what was the last surviving hotel in town from the grand days of America's mineral water boom. Included is the story of the fire and photographs from the fire. A final chapter includes anecdotes and remembrances of events held at the Riverside.

CHAPTER 1

The history of the Riverside Inn begins as a result of a search for oil and an ignored find from that search. Dr. John Hayes Gray was from the Corry area and had come to Cambridge, then called Rockdale, in 1853 to purchase an original 138 acres of land for $1,400 on the northern edge of town. His intentions were to conduct a medical practice and operate a farm. Dr. Gray was not a horse-and-buggy doctor. Instead he traveled on horseback and would go out on the circuit for a week or more before returning home to practice medicine in town. He operated a large farm and hired help to tend to it. According to the 1876 Crawford County Atlas, Dr. Gray's residence was located about the middle of where Gray Alley today meets North Main Street. Gray was quite a forward thinker for the time. Among his ideas, he felt the town should give

ORIGINAL SPRING HOUSE AT CAMBRIDGE SPRINGS SHORTLY AFTER DISCOVERY OF GRAY SPRING BY DR. GRAY.

As more patients came to Cambridgeboro, Dr. Gray improved his spring. He added a tent and a turnstile. One man collected admissions and the other filled the glasses from the spring. (Image from museum collection.)

land for a State Normal School to be built in town. The idea was turned down. The college was built in nearby Edinboro. That was a missed opportunity. Gray also felt that when the railroad was planning on building through town in the early 1860s the tracks should be built closer to the creek. This he felt would keep the town from being cut in half if it were built where the railroad had intended to build. Townspeople scoffed at the idea of Cambridge ever being big enough for the railroad to be a concern. So where did the railroad get built? Right through the middle of town. Dr. Gray was also instrumental in getting the suspension bridge built over French Creek to connect the two sides of town.

One of his successful ideas was prompted by Col. Edwin Drake's first successfully drilled oil well near Titusville in the summer of 1859. Drake had drilled near where oil seeped to the surface and made "oil blossoms" on the surface of the water. As oil fever swept the region, Dr. Gray hoped he might find oil on his property as well. On one particular day, he had set out with a rod to prospect on his land. His family says it was a crowbar, others say he had a sixteen-foot rod which he used to probe the ground. What he eventually found was soft ground in which the rod was fairly easily pushed its full length into the ground. This was along a tributary of French Creek near the Miller Road, the road to Millers Station. When he withdrew the rod, water, not oil, bubbled up. He rushed home for an old gun barrel to case his well. This was later replaced with a penstock. As the water was clearer and cleaner than the water in the tributary and nearby French Creek, Gray left it for his farm help. In the ensuing years the help, as well as other area farmers, drank heavily from the spring with no ill effects.

It was almost another quarter century before the significance of his spring was known. In 1884 Dr. Gray had taken his brother-in-law to Hot Springs, Arkansas, for treatments at the Blue Spring. What he noticed was that the waters there bore a strong resemblance to the waters flowing from his little spring. Upon returning home, Gray sent samples for analysis. The water proved to have high levels of iron and other uncommon properties. Soon he was prescribing the water in large quantities to a few of his chronic cases that had baffled his medical skills. Results were quite satisfying. It wasn't long until his spring and its reputation spread across the United States. Ailments of the

An inspiring view of the sanitarium and hotel from 1893 gives a clear image of the Riverside during the Rider tenure. Rider finished an additional floor on the original sanitarium to the left and completed the east wing to the right. Some of these young maples in front of the hotel were among the final casualties of the fire cleanup operation.
(Image from museum collection.)

With continuing demand for Dr. Gray's treatments, a structure was built across Millers Station Road to replace the tent. Rider had built the first boardwalk to the spring. The **boardwalk bridged the road.** (Image from museum collection.)

stomach, liver, and kidneys were believed to be cured by the consumption of the water. In the coming years, other drilled "springs" of magnesia, lithia, and sulfur were developed throughout the town.

Gray needed to improve his spring now that it was becoming well-known. For those coming to the spring, he began by placing a tent over the spring, placed a turnstile at the entrance, and hired two people to staff the spring: one to collect admission, and one to ladle the water. In a short time, the tent was replaced with a wooden structure and eventually a two-story building was completed for the use of those seeking treatment from the spring water. Gray was also shipping five-gallon jugs of his spring water by rail to his patients.

Two years later, Dr. Gray was prescribing his mineral waters to eager patients coming to the borough. The demand for lodging prompted the organization of the Gray Mineral Fountain Company. Dr. Gray and his

Still on the north side of Millers Station Road, this 1889 structure gave comfort to those coming for the mineral waters. After a quarter mile walk, they were ready for shade and a glass or two of water. (Image from museum collection.)

Mineral Waters
Drinking Code

If at Riverside you'd thrive,
  Drink of water, glasses five;
That is in the morn at ten;
  At four P. M., the same again.

In early morn don't overdo.
  Before breakfast take but two.
When retiring for the night,
  One will make you sleep just right.

You will find it the best thing
  To quaff it sparkling at the Spring.
Rapidly it must be tossed,
  Lest it's makeup should be lost.

૭૦

These directions you may vary
But of enormous drafts be wary.

(Author unknown)

A poem by an unknown poet and from an unknown year spells out the guidelines for patients and guests regarding just how much and how often the mineral waters should be consumed during the day. (Image from museum collection.)

investors organized on July 15, 1886, and raised $50,000 capital to build a first-class hotel and sanitarium. Water was to be piped from the spring to the sanitarium. Modern amenities included 20 bathrooms, a consulting room, two cooling rooms, two large sitting rooms, and two marble-fixtured washrooms in the original 34' x 100' structure which ran parallel to Fountain Avenue. The sanitarium opened for business in May 1887. The original investors were president A. Sherwood (owner of an 1884 sawmill on the creek banks along Main St.), secretary M.B. Ross (maker and seller of Crokinole boards at the Phoenix Novelty Company), treasurer J.O. Sherrod (banker), directors: Dr. J.H. Gray, P.A. Gage, J.B. Wilbur (owner of a hardware and Sayles Opera House), A. Sherwood, M.B. Ross, T.T. Root (building contractor and farmer), and J.L. Docter. The investors were incorporated April 1889. They finished the third floor on the original structure and added an east wing that led toward the creek nearly doubling the hotel's size. May 25, 1889, Dr. Gray leased 1.25 acres north of Millers Station Road to Gray Mineral Water Company to build a drinking and bathing house or pavilions, laying out pleasure grounds, tennis courts and croquet grounds for healthful amusement.

This first sanitarium and hotel was not a huge success. Expenses outstripped income. The hotel property and structure were sold at sheriff sale to be purchased by the Kelly Bank to settle the mortgage. This was not a great start to the mineral water boom to come.

CHAPTER 2

Enter William D. Rider of Franklin. He was a man of vision and saw the possibility of developing a health resort. He sold his assets in Franklin in order to purchase the hotel from the J.L. and A. Kelly Bank and secure the spring and farm lease from Dr. Gray. Under Rider's leadership, the hotel was enlarged. This included the building projects of the casino, bottling works, the barn to the north of the hotel for the hotel's prize Jersey herd, fine horses, and rigs for livery, the quarter mile boardwalk to the Gray Spring over the flood prone pasture, rebuilding the spring house on the south side of Millers Station Road, and adding a large garden to provide fresh produce for the hotel. Salesmen

William Rider was from Franklin. His own health had been poor. After seeing positive results from drinking from Gray's spring, he saw great potential in turning the town into a health resort. He sold his assets in Franklin and used the funds to purchase the sanitarium and hotel property from the Kelly Bank in 1890.

(Image from museum collection.)

were marketing Gray Spring Water in Cleveland, Buffalo, and Pittsburgh.

Dr. Gray died in 1891, leaving behind his wife and seven children. As per the lease agreement, upon Dr. Gray's death, Rider had the option to purchase the Gray's parcels including the Gray Spring for a whopping amount of $60,000. Rider passed on the offer.

Rider had a variety of partners during his tenure with the Riverside. J.W. Winthrop of Titusville bought into the hotel in May 1891 and stayed through June 1892. Roland and Forbes joined the team from August 6, 1892, to December 1893. In a disagreement among the three, Roland was given the option to buy out Rider. When he couldn't raise the funds in nine days, he was forced to sell his share to Rider. With Rider owning the hotel again, new investors were sure to want in. E.Y. Breck of Pittsburgh bought in as a silent partner in 1894, as did town physician, Dr. J.H. Martin, with the condition of becoming the hotel's on-site physician. The old saying of "two's company, three's a crowd" might have been written about this group. Dr. Martin started out doing his job well. After some six months, he was not always easy to find within the hotel complex when he was needed. When confronted about his frequent absences by Rider and Breck, Dr. Martin countered that Rider was spending extravagantly on the hotel and cited the Tally Ho carriage and a $450 painting purchased for the lobby as examples. He also cited Rider's poor handling of a certain card player and his family's tab. The dispute continued to fester until it went to Crawford County court September 1, 1894. After the lengthy testimony of both sides, the judge ruled that due to irreconcilable differences, the partnership would have to be dissolved. The hotel would have to be sold. It was to be advertised in a minimum of three newspapers for two weeks. This attracted the attention of William Baird Sr. formerly of the Keystone Bridge Company of Pittsburgh. His wife had previously indulged in the Cambridge spa's benefits, so he was familiar with the hotel. As Baird was seeking to get out of the bridge business, the Riverside was a perfect opportunity to do just that. Baird closed on the hotel on February 2, 1895. Rider was now without a hotel of his own but not for long. He went to the highest ground in town to build his 300 guest room, brick showplace, the Hotel Rider, which opened in 1897.

Rider saw the advantages of improving the boardwalk to the Gray Spring. It would keep guests from having to walk through the pasture and also be high enough to be above flood waters. The boardwalk extended north from near the hotel's barn to the Gray Spring across Millers Station Road. The walkway was built above the Jersey herd pasture. A halfway rest area was added. Lamp posts supplied light for evening strolls. (Image from museum collection.)

Rider made many improvements during his five-year tenure with the Riverside. He enlarged the hotel and added the Casino. The lower floor of the Casino housed billiards and bowling, and later George Smith's Beauty and Barber Shop. A maple dance floor and stage were on the upper floor. The hotel had its own orchestra to furnish music for dancing every evening in the summer and three evenings a week in the winter. The Casino overlooked the Riverside Park and the boat house where skiffs, canoes, and launches could be rented for an afternoon's entertainment on **French Creek.** (Image from museum collection.)

In this period postcard view of Riverside Park a visitor relaxes at the Riverside's French Creek boat launch while enjoying the scenery from a swing. (Image from museum collection.)

Flooding on French Creek was a serious concern of hotel owners. That is evidenced by this view of the Main Street suspension bridge during a flood likely in 1893. The completed east wing is visible. Absent in the photo is the Casino to the right of the hotel. Dr. Gray had been a proponent of replacing the suspension bridge to better connect the two sides of town. (Image from museum collection.)

This photo from the late 1890s-early 1900s shows the interior of the ballroom at the Casino. It appears to be a group of young adults with the hotel orchestra on stage.
(Image from museum collection.)

What most remember as the tennis courts and lawn to the south by the creek had from the 1890s served as a produce garden for the hotel. It appears that raised beds were popular even then. The pump house brought water from the creek to water the gardens.
(Image from museum collection.)

This postcard image from about 1900 shows the Casino as well as produce and flower gardens. Growing their own was best for the hotel in the years before trucks could deliver fresh produce and flowers. This was taken before the breezeway was built to connect the hotel and Casino. An open-sided breezeway was added to connect the hotel and casino in 1897. (Image from museum collection.)

Rider purchased a stagecoach and named it the Tally Ho. His plan was to use the coach to travel to Erie to pick up hotel patrons from the train station there. In doing this, patrons avoided the train travel to Corry and back to Cambridgeboro. One can only guess at the rough and dusty trip that would have been. Rider also used the Tally Ho to take guests out for riding in the countryside. The coach was pulled by two or four horses. A coachman in livery would sound a four-foot long horn as the coach traveled the area. The ladies in their long dresses and big hats carried their parasols. There would be much horn blowing, talking, and laughing during the outings. (Image courtesy of Joe Ledrick.)

With his purchase of the sanitarium from the Kelly Bank, Rider added a bottling works behind his hotel. Water was piped from the spring a quarter mile away to be bottled in glass and five-gallon pottery containers. Salesmen were promoting the spring water in Cleveland, Pittsburgh, and Buffalo. Train carloads were being shipped to distributors in **those cities.** (Image from museum collection.)

The above photograph comes from a booklet that promotes the Gray Spring. The booklet touts the mineral content of the spring and its healing properties.
(Image from museum collection.)

A new dairy barn was added to the north of the hotel soon after Rider's purchase in 1890. The 60' x 135' structure housed the prize Jersey herd of as many as 60 cattle. The herd provided milk and cream for the hotel's guests. The barn also served as a livery for the hotel's Tally Ho team of horses and guests' horses, and provided shelter for their carriages. As the auto came into vogue, the barn was used as a garage for many guests' **expensive cars.** (Image from museum collection.)

CHAPTER 3

The Baird genealogy traces William Baird's birth in 1847 to the city of Bright located in Ontario, Canada. His heritage was Scottish, and he had seven siblings. Around the age of 20, he left Canada to pursue jobs in United States. He eventually became involved with bridge building and moved to Pittsburgh with the Keystone Bridge Company founded by Andrew Carnegie.

When he married in 1874, it was to Elizabeth Smith, also from Bright, Ontario. They would have four children: Nettie, William A., Maude, and Lillian. Maude died young, but the other siblings would live out their years in Cambridge Springs.

As William's career continued, he was noted for work on several large bridge projects, among these the 6th Street Bridge in Pittsburgh and the Memphis Bridge in Tennessee. He entered into a bridge building partnership in 1874

The patriarch of the Riverside, William Baird and his wife Elizabeth pose for a family portrait. He had brought his ailing wife to the Riverside for treatments at the springs. Having liked the establishment, Baird was quick to jump on the opportunity to purchase the hotel and springs when Rider and his partners were forced into selling the hotel and properties by the court to dissolve the partnership. (Image from museum collection.)

with his brother Andrew. They completed many bridge projects, but sadly, a tragic bridge construction accident happened in June of 1892. The Baird brothers had been contractors on the Licking Bridge project in Covington, Kentucky. While under construction, the bridge collapsed and killed dozens, including two Baird brothers, Andrew and Robert.

Although noted in the field of building bridges, Mr. Baird did not return to bridge work. His wife was ill, and he sought a resort area for her health. He learned that the Hotel Riverside was for sale by Rider, Martin, and Breck. He finalized a sale on February 5, 1895, for $75,000. The sale included all of the improvements that William D. Rider had made (the hotel, the casino, the bottling works, the barn, and the boardwalk.) For the next 51 years the Baird family would own and manage the Hotel Riverside. By 1898, William Baird was able to purchase the Gray Mineral Spring House for $55,000 and the Gray farm for $5,000 from the Gray family heirs. Boardwalk improvements were made for easy access from the hotel to the spring house.

During the first five years of ownership, there were many changes that occurred around town. The year 1897 is remembered for the town changing its name from Cambridgeboro since 1892 to Cambridge Springs and also for the huge fire that destroyed much of the downtown business district. Both events happened the same day: April 1. It also would be the year that the Hotel Rider would open on the south side of town.

In 1899, Mr. Baird's son, William A., would begin working with his father at the Hotel Riverside. A formal agreement was made in 1913 when William A. was given ¼ of the owner and operator title. The official partnership from 1913 to 1921 became known as William Baird and William A. Baird.

Hotel Riverside was doing well. In the 1902 *Cutter's Guide* it was described as "...a hotel where the weary may indeed find rest. No detail has been neglected that could add to its helpfulness in restoring you to perfect health." The 1902 *Cutter's Guide* went on to describe the office, parlor, music room, bedrooms, the casino, the cuisine, the gardens, and the view. At that time in 1902, the hotel was open year round.

In October 1909 when a late-season cyclone damaged the boardwalk, it was completely rebuilt with cement piers alongside of the original. The north

This view shows the barn at a busy moment. Visible in the image are the Riverside's bus to transport guests to and from the train station as well as a young horse to the right. The bus remained in use to 1920 when a new Autobus 25 passenger bus was purchased.

(Image from museum collection.)

An unusual late-season tornado visited the north side of Cambridge Springs on October 21, 1909. In this picture you can see the damage done to the barn by the twister. You may even see a carriage stored on the upper floor of the barn. The hotel's north wing and the boardwalk did not escape the storm's wrath. A section of hotel roof was torn off, and a portion of boardwalk was blown to the ground. Visible in this image can be seen the damaged support posts from the boardwalk. The storm prompted Bairds to rebuild the entire boardwalk using concrete posts replacing the wooden ones.

(Image from museum collection.)

side of the barn was ripped open by the cyclone and had to be repaired.

The Baird family would own and operate the hotel during the growth years of Cambridge Springs, and the Bairds kept pace with many changes and improvements. In 1909, a forty-two foot wide bay window was added to the dining room. The bay featured beveled lead crystal panels across the top to radiate light into the dining room. A cement block ice house was added where 2,500 pounds of ice could be made daily. In 1911 improvements were also made to the mineral spring house.

The availability of the automobile to more Americans began changing visitors' length of stay at the Hotel Riverside. Before widespread automobile use, visitors came for weeks and even the entire summer. The Riverside was a destination. Once people could travel to further destinations by automobile, they did not want to stay so long in one location. Responding to the changes, in 1913, William A. encouraged his father to take the poultry farm land north of town and build a nine hole golf course. A golf course would provide visitors a reason to stay longer or visit more frequently. The course opened in 1915.

Another change occurred in 1918, when they bought a prize-winning Jersey herd and an additional seventy-seven acres a mile and a half south of Cambridge Springs. The herd would provide milk and cream for the hotel's kitchens and guests. The land would provide additional gardens as well as grain for the herd.

An issue with bottling the water at the Hotel occurred in 1916. The Pure Food and Drug Act of 1906 was used by the American Medical Association to crack down on mineral spring resorts. William and his son were sued by the Agriculture Department for misbranding the "Gray Mineral Water." They plead guilty to three charges. The Baird's had labeled the water as "bottled at the source." Actually it was bottled a quarter mile from the spring. It was promoted as "pure spring water," but in fact the water was being carbonated. Also the cures claimed on the label were not supported by medical evidence. The Bairds were found guilty and were fined all of $20.00. Their labels were reworded and business continued.

The Hotel Riverside continued to thrive. Research by local historian Ed Ledrick detailed the vitality of the hotel in the early 1920s. The casino

After the 1909 tornado, the boardwalk was rebuilt using concrete pillars instead of the wood that had been used. Here new columns are being placed along the original boardwalk during reconstruction. (Image from museum collection.)

The second spring house was built on the south side of Millers Station road in 1911. This eliminated the need for the boardwalk to continue to cross above the road. The reconstructed boardwalk conveniently arrived right at the front porch. This structure burned in September 1941. A third spring house was built to replace the lost building. (Image from museum collection.)

featured the ball room, billiards and bowling areas, and George Smith's barber shop. The large barn served multiple purposes including garage space for the new automobiles that visitors were driving into town. Refrigeration and laundry facilities were well equipped. Thermal and public bath rooms were located in the basement of the south wing. There were sleeping rooms and a dining room for employees in the northeast wing (above the kitchen) known as Help's Hall. Boating on French Creek from the boat launch in Riverside Park behind the hotel was also available as well as tennis to the west of the hotel.

William Baird passed away in 1921 after months of failing health. He died at his summer residence at the Hanson Cottage near the corner of Main and McClellan Streets. His original purchase of seven acres had grown over the years to 435 acres in various locations. His contributions to the Hotel Riverside and the town of Cambridge Springs would be carried on by his family for another twenty-five years.

With William's passing, the hotel ownership reorganized to become known as William Baird and Son Company with William A. owning 5/12ths, his mother Elizabeth owning 3/12ths, and sisters Nettie and Lillian each owning 2/12ths. This ownership title would be used until 1933.

William A., who was born in 1877, was 44 when his dad passed away. He had married Jeannette Riggs in 1903. After his marriage, he and Jeannette built a home on McClellan Street adjoining the hotel grounds. A home for Will's mother Elizabeth and his two sisters, Nettie and Lillian, was built across the street from William and Jeannette in 1926. Both homes still stand in 2017.

New opportunities were explored by William Baird and Son Company. In 1923 the golf course expanded to 18 holes, and they broke ground for a new clubhouse which opened in 1924. In the winter of 1924-25, Baird partnered with T.C. Morgan to offer winter sports programs. They hired William Mathews to oversee the construction. For the town, they offered a toboggan sled at both the golf course and the hotel and an ice rink near the Spring House.

In the 1930s Gray Mineral Springs was still active, but the mineral water era was over. When William A.'s mother Elizabeth died in 1933, the hotel reorganized and became known as W. A. Baird and Co. William owned ½, Nettie ¼, and Lillian ¼.

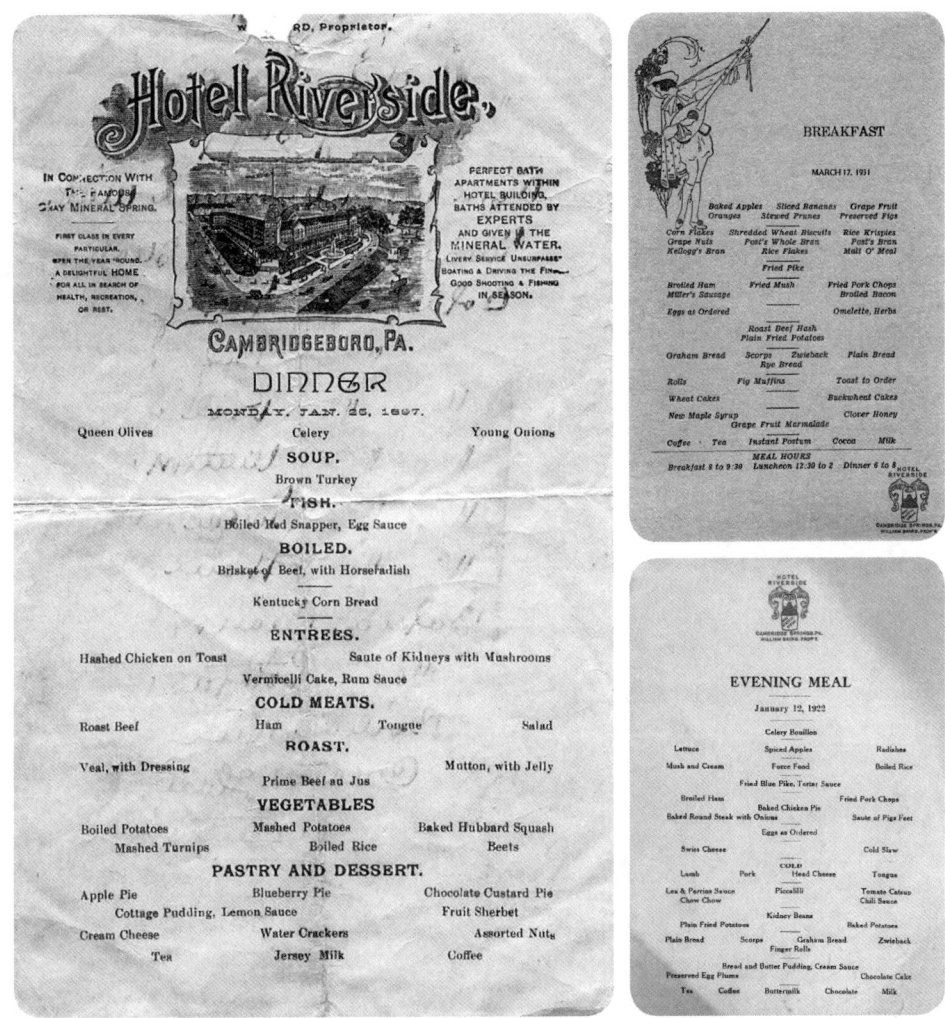

These three menus give an idea of how appetites changed over the years.
(Image from museum collection.)

A fire at the Spring House in 1941 led to another replacement spring house project by the Baird family. During the World War II time frame, the hotel revised their shuttle services for guests going to and from the rail stations, golf course, and springhouse. During the years of war rationing, this was one way to help save on gas and tires for the war effort. When the family decided to leave the hotel business in 1946, the Baird Family had owned and operated the Hotel Riverside and properties for 51 years. This would be the longest period of ownership in the hotel's history. Col. Francis W. Parke would become the new owner and manager.

The Baird family stayed active with organizations and generously supported the town and county. William had a long association with Republican Party. He had been a delegate to the national convention in 1928. In 1953 he was invited to the presidential inauguration for Dwight David Eisenhower. It is not known whether he attended or not. From 1912 on he served as president of the Crawford County Road Association.

In 1951, W. A. Baird donated $5,000 toward a new athletic field for the Cambridge Springs Junior-Senior High School that was being built. In 1953, Nettie and Lillian gave additional money. The dedication of the field and lights was during a night game in 1953. The 1954 Cambridge Springs High School yearbook is dedicated to William A., Nettie, and Lillian Baird. In 1957 the field was officially named Baird Field.

In the months just before the October twister, the main dining room underwent an extreme makeover. This would double the seating capacity to 300. The forty-two foot wide bay window with the leaded glass panels above was added. Structural modifications were made in order to eliminate several of the columns. The wood paneling and remaining posts received a coat of eggshell white enamel. The plaster was done in a buff color up to the white ceiling. Draperies and an aisle carpet of heavy brussels, both in dark green, complemented the scheme. Mission-styled quartersawn oak furniture with leather upholstered chairs, brass chandeliers and sconces, and new linens and table service completed the dining room. (Image from museum collection.)

William A. passed away in 1958, and his wife died ten years later in 1968. Nettie Baird passed in 1972 and her sister, Lillian, in 1973. The Baird family was gone, but the family name would be remembered. The family bequeathed $100,000 to build a town library, and money was also left for the care of Baird Field.

In late 2013, the Heritage Society received a donation of what is believed to have been the desk that William A. Baird utilized during his ownership years of the Hotel Riverside. The Chippendale Revival desk and chair were donated by Denny Atkin. The museum staff had the desk restored by Larry and Kevin Palmiero of Meadville. The desk is on display at the Cambridge Springs Historical Museum. The desk was originally part of the hotel purchase by Col. Parke, but there are no known photographs that show Mr. Baird seated at the desk.

This more recent image shows a more complete view of the bay window in the dining room. (Image from museum collection.)

Hotel Riverside

WM. BAIRD, PROPRIETOR

IN CONNECTION WITH THE FAMOUS
GRAY MINERAL SPRING
OPEN THE YEAR ROUND

PERFECT BATH APPOINTMENTS WITHIN HOTEL
BUILDING BATHS ATTENDED BY EXPERTS
AND GIVEN IN THE MINERAL WATER

A DELIGHTFUL HOME FOR ALL IN SEARCH OF HEALTH RECREATION OR REST. LIVERY SERVICE
UNSURPASSED. BOATING & DRIVING THE FINEST. GOOD SHOOTING & FISHING SEASON.

Cambridge Springs, Pa.

RATES—$2.00 TO $3.50 PER DAY.

WEEKLY RATES UPON APPLICATION

William Baird promoted his hotel with these business cards. Activities listed take advantage of the region's hunting and fishing opportunities. (Image from museum collection.)

Everyone will recognize the front lobby and desk. This postcard seems to be about 1909 before the woodwork was painted. Look closely for the bellhop bench under the steps. The lobby changed little in 100 years. (Image from museum collection.)

The back lobby as seen in an early postcard. Many have asked about the George Washington piece over the fireplace. Because of the similarities of Mission furniture as in the dining room and age of the postcard, it's safe to say the George had been there before 1909. The piece disappeared into storage during the Leavell years to await its return to the Second Empire mantel with the Hallidays. (Image from museum collection.)

In this May 26, 1938, view of the Riverside kitchen, the viewer gets to see what the general public never saw. Though not during the dining hour, the kitchen is set up for efficiency. (Image courtesy of Elizabeth Susan Parke Brown.)

This second kitchen view from May 27, 1938, appears to be the end of the kitchen at the servers' station. From coffee urns, water glasses, and tray to the small stove in the corner, the items seem to indicate server station. The mixing bowl on the work table shows the viewer that it is still in the kitchen. (Image courtesy of Elizabeth Susan Parke Brown.)

The August 2, 1912, Enterprise News reported of the completion of the handsome arch that was erected at the boardwalk. Large wood pillars topped with arches and finished with scrollwork featured "Gray and Magnesia Springs" on one side and "Gray: The Spring that made Cambridge" on the other. (Image from museum collection.)

Flooding on French Creek was a frequent visitor to Cambridge Springs as well. This photo clearly demonstrates one of the reasons why the elevated boardwalk was built as it was: to allow patrons passage to the Spring House above any floods. (Image from museum collection.)

Riverside Park had quite a visitor for July 4, 1913. The Thomas Brothers aviators of Bath, NY, had pilot Wilson H. Minnerly in town for two flights. The 11:00 flight was delayed until 2:30 to allow time to assemble the plane. The first flight lasted 15 minutes. The second flight at 6:00 proved to be more exciting. Minnerly flew to 2,500 feet and into the face of an approaching thunderstorm. The plane disappeared behind a cloud for ten minutes before reappearing to complete the show. Notice the boardwalk in the background.

(Image courtesy of Sandy Porter.)

With the mineral water craze beginning to wane and the automobile becoming available to more people, the changing times were beginning to impact the hotels in town. The Bairds began to look for ways to diversify. In 1915 they opened the first nine holes of a Riverside Golf Course. The nine holes are what are today's back nine located along Old Rt. 86. This still existing structure was the first pro shop.

(Image from museum collection.)

As golf was gaining in popularity, Bairds chose to add the additional nine holes which opened in 1923. Where the former Bone Hotel sat is today the ninth green. The Bone Hotel represented the only known case of arson among the Cambridge Springs community.

(Image from museum collection.)

The Riverside had its own source for fresh eggs and poultry. Located along route 19 north of town, the chicken farm seen here gave way to development of the additional nine holes for the golf course that opened in 1923. The new clubhouse sat about where the chicken house had been.

(Image from museum collection.)

The Bairds broke ground for the new clubhouse in 1923. The structure, designed by C. Paxton Cody, had a tea room in the right wing, showers and lockers in the left wing, and a main lobby in the center that faced out over the links. Passing through the lobby, golfers crossed a broad circular piazzo to reach the first tee. The clubhouse opened late April 1924. The first image is the architect's design for the front elevation. The second is a photograph of the completed clubhouse. Builders created the clubhouse very close to what the architect had in mind.

(First image courtesy of Elizabeth Susan Parke Brown. Second image from the museum collection.)

Golfers prepare to tee off from the 10th hole at the Riverside Golf Course. The newly completed clubhouse stands in the background. (Image courtesy of Elizabeth Susan Parke Brown.)

The Riverside had its own horsedrawn "bus" that would meet guests at the train station and deliver them to the hotel. This was only one of many buses from the numerous hotels in town that would meet the trains. Baird Sr. loved the old bus. In 1918 the bus was taken to Erie over the winter to be repainted. The building where it was being repaired burned to the ground. When Baird Jr. was called in the morning with the news of the fire, he was delighted to know the old coach was gone. His enthusiasm quickly faded upon receiving another call later in the day. The hotel's bus had been completed just the day before and removed to a storage facility. The bus hadn't burned after all. It was returned to Cambridge Springs to serve the hotel two more years before being sidelined. As reported in the May 10, 1920, *Enterprise News*, "The Riverside has a perfectly beautiful new Autobus, all black and fine outside finish, black inside and leather draperies. It will carry about 25 persons and is a wonderful addition to the hotel." (Image from museum collection.)

Young William A. Baird had served as vice president and Chairman of the Board of the First National Bank for many years. With his father's passing after a long illness in 1921, he and his sisters Lillian and Nettie continued to operate the hotel until 1946. At the time of the sale, the Bairds set up a fund to develop sports at the high school. They also gave money for construction of the high school football field that bears their name.

(Image from museum collection.)

Sisters Nettie and Lillian Baird worked alongside their brother William A. in the hotel. Their brother built a summer home for the sisters and his widowed mother in 1926 near the hotel. His own home was and is still located along McClellan St. just before the hotel property.

(Image courtesy of Rose Smith.)

During the years the Bairds operated the hotel, situations occurred which prompted the legal name of the company to change. The public never really noticed the changes except in the names on the quart crock jugs that were filled and left at the guest room doors in the morning. The Hotel Riverside jug may well have been from the Rider era. From 1895-1913, the jugs bore the name of William Baird, sole owner of the company. Baird's son, William A., became partner with his father from 1913 to William's death in 1921. During this time the jugs were imprinted with William Baird & W.A. Baird. The company reorganized in 1921 after Baird Sr. passed. It was then known as William Baird & Son Company until 1933. A final reorganization changed the name one last time in 1933. The new name was W.A. Baird & Company. For those lucky enough to own one of the various jugs, this will help to date them. (Image courtesy of Gene and Jean Cady.)

In this later view of the front entrance, notice the 1897 addition of a breezeway to the Casino that is now in place. It is still open-sided to allow the breezes to pass.
(Image from museum collection.)

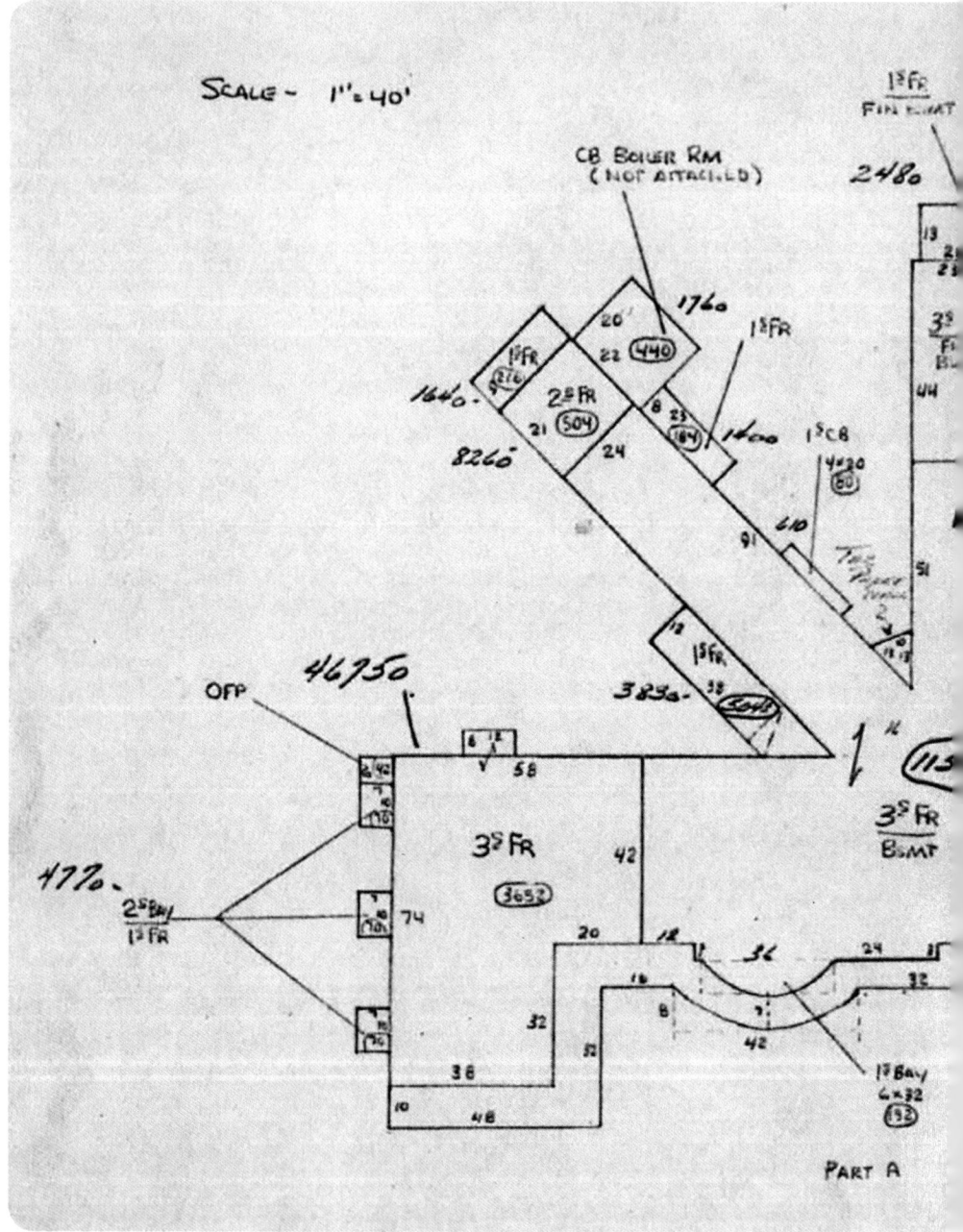

This 1976 map shows the dimensions of the hotel in all its immenseness. By 1946 when the Bairds sold the hotel, the total square footage was 522,020 square feet. The diagonal portion to the upper left had the kitchens and boiler room on the first floor and housing for employees on the upper floors in what was called Help Hall. The Casino/ball room and dinner theater were to the upper right.

(Map used with permission of the Crawford County Planning Commission.)

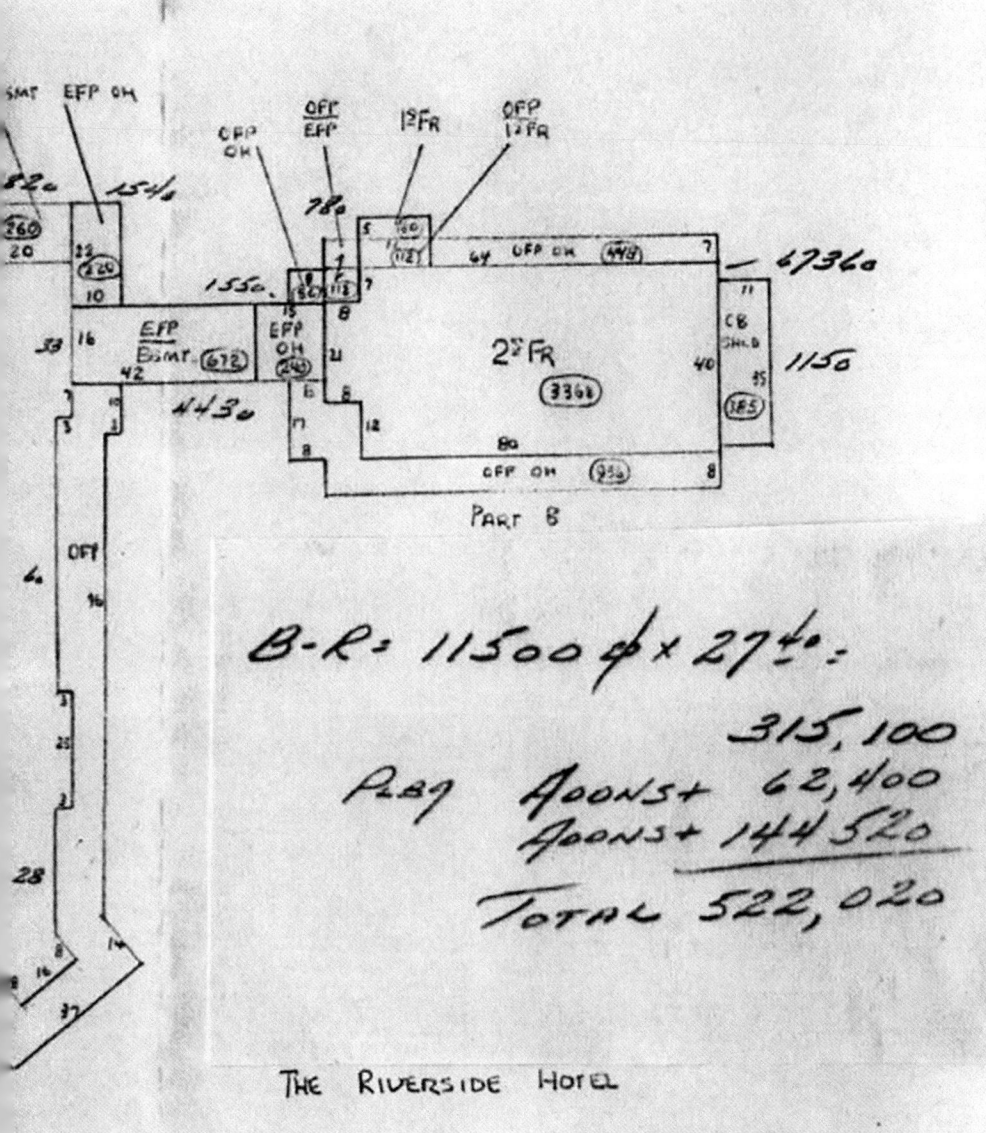

PART B

B-R= 11500 φ × 27½ =

315,100

P₂Bq 4,000s+ 62,400
       4,000s+ 144,520

TOTAL 522,020

THE RIVERSIDE HOTEL

After his 1903 marriage to Jeanette Riggs, William A. Baird had this Colonial Revival home built as his own private residence. It was, and is, on property adjoining the Riverside on McClellan Street. Photographed in 2017. (Image courtesy of Jesse Cornwell.)

This 1926 home on McClellan Street near the hotel was built by William A. Baird for his widowed mother and sisters as a summer home. Photographed in 2017.

(Image courtesy of Jesse Cornwell.)

CHAPTER 4

On August 13, 1946, the Baird family of William, his wife Jeannette, and his two sisters Lillian and Nettie, owners of the Riverside Hotel and golf course sold their hotel and golf course to the Incas Company of Pittsburgh. The hotel had been owned by the Baird family since 1895, a tenure of fifty-one years. The transaction was handled by L. W. Monteverde, a Pittsburgh real estate dealer.

The Incas Company was an incorporated business whose members included Col. Francis W. Parke, Ruth G. Parke, and Clifford Ball. The Incas Company's president and managing director, Col. Francis W. Parke, would operate the hotel. William Baird would continue his association with the hotel in an advisory capacity. Working with J.L. Salen, who had been in management of the hotel for the past twenty years, and Bill Kane, golf professional at the

Col. Francis W. Parke's family portrait from 1904. Francis is on the left.
(Image courtesy of Ed Gifford.)

Riverside Golf Course for the past twenty-two years, Parke intended to open the following May 15.

The hotel property, originally seven acres, now included more than 450 acres with the hotel, surrounding gardens, a Jersey dairy farm, 18 hole golf course, seventy-five acre fruit and vegetable farm, and the famed Gray Mineral Springs.

Col. Francis W. Parke was the son of William Brush Parke and Mary Lucy Hall, and was born on March 7, 1897, in Manhattan, New York. He started in the hotel business washing dishes at the age of fifteen. In 1915 he worked at an Adirondack resort in New York called the Mohawk. His military career began in 1916. After he finished high school, he enlisted into the Army with the 10th NY Infantry where he fought to defend the U.S. / Mexican border from the raids of Pancho Villa's army. After returning to New York for a short time, he was called for World War I combat duty with the 61st Pioneer Infantry serving in St. Mihiel and the Meuse-Argonne. He returned to the United States from France in 1919 and was promoted to First Lieutenant of the U. S. Reserve Officers Corps.

He took a job with the Childs Company in 1926, managing their top NYC Fifth Avenue restaurant. At the age of thirty-one, he was hired by the American Hotel Corporation to manage the Colonial Hotel in Gardner, Massachusetts, for two years. His next move was with wife Ruth (Gerber) and ten week old son Robert to the Baron Steuben Hotel in Corning, New York. A total of ten hotels would come under his management in the next twelve years. He found his life's work was to bring economic health back to ailing hotels. He gained the nickname Scrapper by his brother and friends.

When recalled to military service in World War II as a Captain, Francis Parke resigned as president and manager of the Hotel Henry in Pittsburgh. He was soon promoted to the rank of Major at Camp Lee, Virginia. He was later promoted to Lieutenant Colonel and given command of the Southeast recreation and leave areas. While en route to this post, he and the 37th Infantry was involved in combat in Manilla.

While stationed in the Philippines, Lt. Col. Parke wrote to his friend James J. Johnston, president of the Pennsylvania Hotel Association (PHA), about

Col. Parke, as he preferred to be called, served in the military during WWI and safely returned from France in 1919. He also fought to protect the American border during the Mexican-American War against Francisco "Pancho" Villa in 1915.

(Image courtesy of Elizabeth Parke Brown.)

Lorenzo Bautista and his association of owners of hotels, clubs, restaurants, and bars. He felt their plans for reconstruction of hotels and restaurants in the Philippines would need help from the United States. He requested that they be given access to all PHA facilities. PHA's lists of manufacturers could help with equipment, furnishings, and business practices to aid with the rehabilitation. Lt. Col. Parke was appointed representative of the PHA to assist in any way humanly possible with Mr. Bautista's plans to rebuild the cities and further the partnership between the United States and the Philippines.

Returning to Pittsburgh in 1946, Col. Parke found that his services at the Hotel Henry were no longer needed. The hotel was slated for demolition to make way for a new U.S. Steel building. Hearing of the availability of the Riverside Hotel, he made a decision to purchase the Riverside Hotel properties sight unseen.

When Col. Parke bought the Riverside Hotel lock, stock, and barrel, he did not know it included a working Jersey dairy farm. Despite knowing nothing about Jersey cattle, he had to act as head herdsman for more than a year until finding someone for the job. He soon realized that the hotel and the dairy herd were inseparable, as the herd supplied fresh cream and milk for the guests.

The Riverside Hotel had long been famous for the rich, creamy milk and farm fresh produce grown on the seventy-five acre vegetable and fruit farm it owned and operated. It was stated by Col. Parke that the guests consumed more than 10,000 ears of home grown corn in a year.

After many offers, Col. Parke sold their champion Jersey bull named Victor Gallant Pogis to the New York State College of Agriculture at Cornell in May 1947. The bull had been designated the highest indexed Jersey bull in 1944 in the state of Pennsylvania. The bull was originally purchased by William Baird as a calf and raised at the Riverside Hotel's barn. The bull improved the herd with larger frames, heavier weight, increased milk production, and a more grayish tinge mixed with their Jersey's tan coat.

The dairy herd won many ribbons for high butterfat content of the milk. In 1951 the fifty-five head purebred registered Jersey herd set a record for producing more than 25,000 pounds of butterfat. This was an all-time record for the herd which dated back to 1895.

During 1938, eight years before assuming the role of Riverside manager, this photograph captured Parke with his wife Ruth and son Robert. Parke spent his early life in the military, and he served once again in WWII. (Image courtesy of Elizabeth Parke Brown.)

A young Janet Cook Derrington out for a sleigh ride with her driver Bill in 1950.
(Image courtesy of Janet Derrington.)

This butterfat milk allowed a fifty-six year old tradition of the hotel serving a dish of cornmeal mush with thick, golden cream with each dinner. Cornmeal mush is made by mixing cornmeal, water, and salt in a saucepan, cooking over medium heat, and stirring frequently until it thickens, about 6-7 minutes. If used as a cereal, it is spooned into bowls and served with milk and sugar.

Col. Parke's favorite bedtime drink was a Jersey Highball which consisted of a glass of pure, rich milk straight from the Jersey cow.

A year after the hotel purchase, Col. Parke announced that all employees of the hotel, golf course, farm, mineral springs, thermal and massage baths, recreation hall, and the power house were to be covered by group insurance underwritten by Metropolitan Life Insurance Company. The features of the policy were life insurance of $1,000, weekly sickness and accident benefit of $10, a daily hospital benefit of $5, and allowances for surgical operations from $10 to $150.

The Inn operated year round by offering winter packages of outdoor sports. These included ice skating, on a newly built rink, skijoring (a winter sport where a person is pulled on skis by a horse, dog or vehicle), toboggan slide, trap shooting, and hay and sleigh rides. An old fashioned square dance was held every Saturday in the Casino ballroom.

Parke offered a $15 weekend package. This included meals, lodging, and recreation for one person from Friday night through Sunday afternoon. Unlike most hotels, breakfast had no deadline. Patrons could eat at their convenience in the dining room, at the snack bar, or in bed. It was referred to as a country inn, a trip to grandfather's farm working to maintain the Inn's old charm and dignity. It was soon referred to as a warm, friendly country inn where you could get blissful sleep and farm fresh food. Col. Parke maintained a military kind of order with strict policy of lights out and no noise after 11:00 p.m. for occupants of rooms and suites.

During the Christmas season, the Inn offered a three day holiday package that included transportation to and from Pittsburgh on chartered buses, a room, eight meals, pancake parties, afternoon teas, and fireside snacks. Guests could also assist with decorating the Inn's Christmas tree.

Col. Parke was editor of the Riverside News, a monthly newsletter that was

This great view from the late 1950s shows part of the hotel's Jersey herd in the pasture beneath the boardwalk. The herd was sold at auction on November 30, 1961. The herd numbered 60 cattle. It was determined that the fresh milk from the herd was no longer necessary as dairy products could be readily purchased for the hotel.
(Image from museum collection.)

The swimming pool was added to the hotel grounds adjacent to the barn in 1959. This photo was taken not long after the pool was completed. (Image from museum collection.)

mimeographed and mailed to several thousand past guests each month. He encouraged people to recline, relax, and rest. He stressed that vacations were essential to good health. He would write, "Give yourself a break. Take a Holiday."

In 1947 at a ceremony of the Army Reserve outfit at Webster Hall Hotel in Pittsburgh, Lt. Col. Francis W. Parke assumed command of Headquarters Detachment of the 475th Quartermaster Group.

In 1958 George Sharf was named manager of the Inn by Col. Parke. Sharf came from the Emerson Hotel in Baltimore, Maryland. His hotel training was earned working in his family owned hotel, the Hotel Gettysburg in Gettysburg, PA. He had held executive positions in Cleveland, OH; Jamestown, NY; and Conneaut Lake, PA. Delight N. Cook, secretary to Col. Parke, would be his assistant.

Updates were happening at the hotel and out at the golf course. In 1959 excavation began on a modern swimming pool in the area between the barn and meeting room. The pool opened later that summer. The old mingled with the new as antiques shared space with movie projectors and TV sets. The clubhouse was being remodeled, enlarged, and modernized.

In September 1961 a letter was written by Col. Parke to the Cambridge Springs Borough Council and the editor of the local paper, the *Enterprise*. He had been denied an application to close Fountain Avenue so the Inn could add a covered entrance for arriving and departing guests. This would have featured an enlarged, paved, landscaped, and lighted parking area. He found it difficult to understand why the borough council members were in opposition to helping businesses when it meant "more taxes, more jobs, more general business: a better town and cost nothing?" In the editorial he stated, "The world has changed in its ideas of vacation, and today Rome or Calcutta is just as likely a spot in which Clevelanders or Pittsburghers or Buffalonians can spend their holidays. We have to compete with all other attractions, and we have been successful in doing so because of our program of progress. We are continually planning to make the Riverside a better resort with more facilities of every description."

On November 20, 1961, the 60 cattle of the hotel's Jersey herd went on the auction block. Col. Parke had decided he could no longer afford to keep the cows. A *Pittsburgh Press* article quoted Col. Parke as saying, "Today's economics forced us to sell." All the dairy equipment, stanchions, machinery, 5,000 bales of hay, 300 bales of wheat straw, 500 bushels of oats, and 100 bushels of corn were auctioned. Col. Parke made plans to build a carriage house annex of 28 rooms, to connect it to the Inn and to the 60 x 135 foot barn, and construct a new 9-hole golf course with par 3 holes in the former pasture. The annex was never started, but a par 3 golf course was built in the pasture under the boardwalk.

In 1962 the newest thing at the Inn was a 120 foot long drip dry tennis court. It was designed with a correct fall of one inch to each ten feet for immediate drainage following rain and a true bounce surface that was painted green. Two more tennis courts were planned before July 4th, but these were never completed.

Col. Parke's farm, shown on this postcard from 1970, provided produce for the Inn.
(Image courtesy of William Gifford.)

The Inn was now known primarily as a vacation spot featuring its 18 hole regulation size golf course and an 9 hole par 3 course. The golf courses had 16,000 rounds of golf played in 1963.

Col. Parke had a rare collection of mustache cups that were on display in locked glass display cases in the back lobby of the Inn near the fireplace. He had bought several cups at a sale and added one now and then. Soon it became a hobby. The twenty-some cups came from all over the country. Many had been gifts from friends or Riverside guests. The mustache cups were used during a time when men wore flowing and bushy mustaches. The design was intended to keep the contents of the cup from getting into the mustache and vice versa.

The most rare of his mustache cups was a cup designed for left-handed men. In this case the bridge of the cup is to the right of the cup handle. After years of searching, a left-handed cup was added to Col. Parke's collection by Ralph Matee, executive of the Warren Telephone Company in Warren, Ohio, who found a Capo de Monte left handed cup made in Italy in a shop at the Willard Hotel in Washington, D.C.

Starting in 1963, the Inn would no longer be kept open during the winter. For the closing weekend in October, the Inn hosted a huge Halloween Gala party with over 200 guests. The Inn could not house all the guests that wanted to come, so local motels helped house guests. Actually the celebration was for its final season under Col. Parke's ownership. He had sold the Inn and was bidding them farewell.

The Riverside Inn was sold for $500,000 to Royston Laboratories and the North Suburban Land Company of Pittsburgh in December 1963.

Col. Parke then retired to his farm south of Cambridge Springs. Here he continued to maintain a monthly newsletter about his farm and other activities. In 1973 he was married to Betty Charley. They moved to Belknap, New Hampshire, to live his remaining years. Betty's family was there.

Lt. Col. Francis "Scrapper" Parke died in Belknap, New Hampshire, on March 5, 1992, at the age of ninety-four. He is buried in Arlington National Cemetery, Arlington, Virginia.

Col. Francis W. Parke
(Image courtesy of Elizabeth Parke Brown.)

Frank Parke's Special Guest Events

Throughout his ownership of the Riverside Inn, Frank Parke, known by everyone as Colonel Parke, catered to the needs of his guests. Each one was special to him.

Tuesday evenings were known as the hot dog/hamburger cookouts. These were located on the lawn near the gardens. Colonel would don his white chef's hat, white chef's coat and barbecue, and with a flourish, cook tasty morsels for each guest.

Saturday evenings found him in the grand ballroom, showing old time movies. Chairs were arranged theater style and popcorn was served. The old reels would then roll, displaying such movies as "It Happened One Night" with Clark Gable and Claudette Colbert.

Christmas was always a special time for the Colonel and guests. Reservations were made far in advance to spend the holidays at the grand old hotel. The festivities would begin Christmas Eve with each guest helping to decorate the big tree in the front lobby. When the tree stood in all its glory, egg nog/hot chocolate would be served. After all had retired, the Colonel would get out stockings and label each with a guest's name. They were then hung with care in the long hallway leading to the back lounge. Each was quickly filled with a special gift and other goodies to be opened on Christmas morning.

Growing Up Years at the Old Riverside Inn

As a young child it was always fun to play games and "hike" with friends in the back meadow of the hotel. As usual, when we were told to stay away from a certain area, that it was dangerous; well, then we did exactly what we were told not to do. For example a small creek in the aforementioned meadow overflowed and was quite deep as it flowed directly into the river.

The old barn always held such great mystery and enticement. The loft especially created a wonderful playground, complete with fresh hay smells and lot of ropes to swing down into fresh straw that was being stored for the winter. In the lower barn level, one got to pet the cows, brush them and even once in a while play at milking them. Once a dare was made to ride one, and of course I was caught, punished, etc. Fortunately, the young cow suffered no ill effect from this event.

During the winter months, the hotel toboggan run captured the attention of all. Exhaustion, freezing, and elation were words to describe how we felt at the end of a great day on the big sled!

As one grew older, the old wooden boardwalk connecting the hotel grounds to the mineral spring offered wonderful strolls after a date! It was quite the busy place for many high school students.

I worked to earn extra money being the hotel pool lifeguard. This went on, of course, until several high school friends opted to plan an unauthorized pool party. This event was interrupted by the night security guard and entailed all sorts of ramifications. Consequences were initiated much to the chagrin of all present.

Senior Prom night came with a very special Hotel Riverside extravaganza. Ten young people were invited to dinner in the grand dining room prior to the prom. All were dressed in lovely prom dresses and the boys in suits with matching flower boutonnières. The five course meal was elegant and very lovely as the hotel assistant administrator had handled every detail!

Then came the big graduation day and a career in nursing becoming even more of a reality. August soon found one leaving the hotel to live in Philadelphia and pursue a career in nursing.

Trips continued to be made back to the hotel to visit family and former high school friends. Somehow it was never quite the same again though. However, fond memories of Hotel Riverside will remain in my heart.

- Janet Cook Derrington

RIVERSIDE NEWS

MARCH - 1951   THE RIVERSIDE INN - CAMBRIDGE SPRINGS, PA.   PHONE 2981

SPRING. THESE ARE MILD SPRING DAYS. NO REAL TOUCH OF SUMMER YET; JUST A SOFT PAUSE BETWEEN THE SEASONS, GIVING YOU THE BEST OF BOTH. NOT TOO COLD, AS IT HAS BEEN; NOT TOO WARM, AS IT WILL BE . . . . THIS IS THE TIME OF YEAR OUR OLD GUESTS LOVE BEST. "RID UP" TO USE THE OLD EXPRESSION IS THE ORDER OF SPRINGTIME. FENCES TO BE REPAIRED; LAWNS TO BE RAKED, ROLLED AND LIMED; LITTER TO BE GATHERED UP AND BURNED; PRUNING TO GET ON WITH; PLOWING TO BE DONE; ROSE TRELLISES TO BE FASTENED UP AND STRAW COVERINGS REMOVED; ROADS TO BE SCRAPED AND GRADED; GOLF GREENS TO BE TREATED AND WORKED OVER; MOWERS TO BE SHARPENED. YES, SPRING IS TRULY A TIME OF CLEAN-UP AND PREPARATION FOR THE BIG SEASON AHEAD. INDIVIDUALS TOO, CAN RID THE COBWEBS FROM THEMSELVES BY A VISIT TO RIVERSIDE. COUNTRY AIR, SUNSHINE, FARM-FRESH FOOD, ALL HELP A PERSON TO PREPARE FOR TASKS AHEAD IN THE DAY TO DAY BUSINESS OF LIVING.

PUZZLE TABLE. A KING-SIZE SQUARE TABLE HAS BEEN CONSTRUCTED AND WILL SOON BE INSTALL-ED ON THE L-SUN PORCH WITH A VERY LARGE JIG-SAW PUZZLE. THIS PERMANENT INSTALLATION WILL OFFER TO ALL WHO PASS, A CHALLENGE TO TRY THEIR SKILL.

NEW PIEL CHAIRS FOR ALL GUEST ROOMS ARE NOW FULLY INSTALLED. THESE COOL, COMFORTABLE, WOVEN GRASS CHAIRS WERE MADE IN CHINA AND HAVE BEEN POPULAR FOR MANY YEARS.

JOE GILLETTE OUR SMILING, NIGHT MAN IS LOOKING FORWARD TO VISITING HIS GRANDCHILDREN IN CLEVELAND OVER A LONG WEEK-END ON HIS WIFE'S 72ND. BIRTHDAY. HAVE A FINE HOLIDAY, JOE, AND BE SURE TO COME BACK!

OLD FASHIONED STRAWBERRY SHORTCAKE HASN'T MISSED AN APPEARANCE AT SUNDAY DINNER FOR THE PAST FIVE YEARS. IT'S POPULARITY IS EASILY UNDERSTOOD. FLUFFY, SWEET; BAKING POWDER BISCUITS, FRESH FROM THE OVEN, ARE SPLIT AND FILLED WITH LUSCIOUS, FRESH STRAWBERRIES IN THEIR OWN SYRUP. ANOTHER SPOONFUL ON THE TOP LAYER, THEN OVER ALL A GENEROUS MOUND OF THICK, JERSEY, WHIPPED CREAM. IT'S ALL SMACKING GOOD.

GRACIOUS LIVING, IT IS SAID, IS FADING AWAY INTO THE DEAR, DEAD PAST. WE CAN'T QUITE BELIEVE THIS TO BE WHOLLY TRUE. AT RIVERSIDE MANY OLD CUSTOMS; THE NICER SERVICES; THE QUIET GENTILITY; THE KINDLY COURTESIES ARE STILL MUCH IN EVIDENCE. WE HOPE THEY MAY LIVE ON FOR MANY, MANY YEARS TO COME.

BOWLING AND ALL THE OTHER ACTIVITIES OF THE RECREATION HALL ARE ALL AVAILABLE AGAIN AFTER BEING CLOSED FOR THE WINTER. IT'S GOOD TO HEAR THE BALLS ROLL AND THE LAUGHTER OF GUESTS AS THEY HAVE FUN AT THESE INDOOR SPORTS.

BILL KANE HAS SENT WORD THAT HE'LL BE ON THE JOB AGAIN AS GOLF PROFESSIONAL THE FIRST WEEK IN APRIL. THIS WILL BE HIS 28TH. CONSECUTIVE YEAR AS AN OUTSTANDING GOLF TEACHER AT OUR COURSE. PLAN TO COME SOON AND LET BILL TAKE OUT THE KINKS IN YOUR PLAY.

GOLF COURSE WILL OPEN ANY DAY JUST AS QUICKLY AS THE SOIL FIRMS ENOUGH. YOU'RE BOUND TO HAVE SOME PLAY SO, COME ALONG.

DEMIJOHN. WE FOUND UP IN THE ATTIC A WONDERFUL ANTIQUE JUG. IT'S OF HUGE PROPORTIONS AND PROBABLY HOLDS 5 GALLONS. IT'S HEAVY AS THE MISCHIEF. GREY IN COLOR WITH BROWN AND BLUE MARKINGS. IT STANDS ABOUT 18 INCHES HIGH. WE'VE ALREADY DESIGNED A HUGE LAMP TO BE CREATED FROM IT; THAT OVERALL WILL BE ABOUT 40 INCHES HIGH. WHAT A LAMP IT WILL BE FOR OUR BIG, ROUND, BLACK WALNUT TABLE IN THE LOUNGE.

FLOYD MOSBACHER WILL PRESIDE AT THE MINERAL SPRINGS AGAIN THIS YEAR WHICH MARKS THE 92ND. ANNIVERSARY OF THE DISCOVERY BY DR. GRAY OF HIS HEALTH GIVING IRON WATER. BEST "SPRING TONIC" THERE IS!

RATES. WE HAVE AGAIN CHECKED OTHER RESORTS AND FIND THAT WE CONTINUE TO HAVE THE LOWEST RATE SCHEDULES OF ALL. SLIGHT ADVANCES WERE MADE OF COURSE, BUT THEY STILL REPRESENT A HEAP OF VALUE.

SPRING RATES ARE IN EFFECT UNTIL MAY 13TH. ASK FOR A COMPLETE SCHEDULE FOR YOURSELF OR FRIENDS.

SHALL WE SEE YOU SOON?

CORDIALLY,

Frank Parke

Newsletter from March 1951.

(Image courtesy of Elizabeth Parke Brown.)

60

RIVERSIDE NEWS

FEBRUARY – 1956   THE RIVERSIDE INN – CAMBRIDGE SPRINGS, PA.   PHONE 2981

HICKORY NUTS FROM OUR TREES IN THE MEADOW AND PICKED UP BY OUR GUESTS LAST FALL ARE NOW BEING FED TO OUR BIG GREY SQUIRRELS. A GENEROUS SUPPLY IS KEPT HANDY FOR THEM ON THE MAIN PORCH AND THEY MAKE REGULAR TRIPS FOR THEIR DINNERS. IT'S PROBABLY A PROBLEM TO PROVIDE PROVENDER WITH HEAVY SNOWS LYING ON THE GROUND.

AFTERNOON TEA AND CAKES WITH OUR COMPLIMENTS IS ALWAYS POPULAR ON SATURDAY AFTERNOONS. IT IS A PLEASANT INTERLUDE WHICH PRESENTS ANOTHER OPPORTUNITY FOR CHIT-CHAT AND HELPS OUR GUESTS TO BECOME BETTER ACQUAINTED WITH THE STAFF AND OTHER GUESTS.

WILLIAM H. TRITSCH IS OUR NEW ASSISTANT MANAGER WHO'LL KEEP AN EAGLE EYE ON THE FOOD AND BEVERAGE OPERATION AMONG OTHER RESPONSIBILITIES. WITH HIS CHARMING WIFE, THEY HAVE JUST ARRIVED AFTER THE LIEUTENANT SERVED TWO YEARS ON ACTIVE DUTY WITH THE AIR FORCE. THEY ARE GRADUATES OF PENN STATE UNIVERSITY AND HAIL FROM BUTLER AND PITTS-BURGH RESPECTIVELY. YOU'LL SEE THEM ABOUT AND FIND THEM ANXIOUS TO BE OF HELP WHEN YOU ARE HOLIDAYING AT THE RIVERSIDE.

GOLF'S KNOCKING AT THE DOOR. IN JUST A FEW MORE WEEKS, APRIL WILL BE HERE AND WE'RE OPTIMISTIC THAT THE WEATHER WILL BE SO GOOD THAT YOU'LL GET IN A HEAP OF APRIL GOLF. PLANS CALL FOR CLUBHOUSE OPENING ON FRIDAY, APRIL 20TH. BOB ACKER WILL BE BACK AS MANAGER AND MARGARET WILL HELP YOU TO SOME OF HER DEE-LICIOUS FOODS. BILL KANE OPENS HIS PRO SHOP AND MARIE KANE WILL HAVE CADDIES AVAILABLE ON SATURDAY, APRIL 14TH.

RALPH GUESMAN IS GETTING ALL EQUIPMENT READY TO MAKE THE COURSE IN BEAUTIFUL CON-DITION. HIS YOUNG, FRIENDLY SMILE HAS ALREADY MADE HIM MANY FRIENDS IN THE FEW MONTHS HE'S BEEN HERE. HIS EXPERIENCE IN OHIO, ILLINOIS AND WESTERN NEW YORK STATE MAKES HIM ESPECIALLY WELL FITTED FOR HIS NEW RESPONSIBILITIES AS GREENSKEEPER OF THE RIVERSIDE. WE KNOW THAT WE SHALL BE PROUD OF RALPH AND HIS WORK HERE.

FARMERS ARE REAL GAMBLERS WHO MAKE THE FELLOWS AT LAS VEGAS LOOK LIKE PIKERS. THOSE BOYS BET ON HORSES, CARDS OR DICE. BUT ANY FARMER STICKING TO HIS FURROW YEAR AFTER YEAR IS A GENUINE GAMBLER. HE BETS ON WEATHER AND THAT'S ONE GAME THAT CAN'T BE FIXED. HURRICANES OR DROUGHTS, THE FARMER NEVER KNOWS HOW HIS CROPS WILL FARE. THE ONLY REASON WE STAY AT IT IS TO BE SURE THAT YOU HAVE A HEAP OF FARM-FRESH FOOD WHILE YOU ARE ON A RIVERSIDE HOLIDAY.

OUR JERSEY HERD IS NOW INCREASED TO 62 HEAD. SOME 32 ARE MILKING AND GIVING THE HEAVIEST MILK IN THE WORLD. AND THE CREAM! DON'T BELIEVE THERE IS ANOTHER PLACE WHICH PUTS A LARGE SILVER PITCHER OF HEAVY CREAM ON YOUR TABLE AND SAYS, "HELP YOURSELF!"

THE VERNAL EQUINOX IS SOON AT HAND. ON MARCH 20TH. AT 10:21 IN THE MORNING, WINTER IS FINISHED AND SPRING ARRIVES. MARCH WEATHER IS SUPPOSED TO BE WARMER WITH LESS PRE-CIPITATION THAN CUSTOMARY FOR THIS USUALLY STORMY MONTH. PACIFIC STATES, HOWEVER, ARE PROMISED ANOTHER BATCH OF HEAVY RAINS ABOUT MARCH 8TH.

BLACK EBONY IS THE NEW FINISH WHICH OUR MASTER DECORATOR, GEORGE BRINK, IS GIVING OUR DINING ROOM FURNITURE. IT'S LOOKING VERY SMART AND GAY, YET DIGNIFIED.

BROILED TENDERLOIN STEAK. A BIG STEER OF 1,000 POUNDS GOES TO MARKET AND WHEN HE'S ALL DIVIDED UP FOR THE GOURMETS, THERE'S ONLY ABOUT FIFTEEN POUNDS OF CHOICE TENDER-LOIN AVAILABLE. WE TAKE A BEAUTIFUL SLICE OF THIS TENDERLOIN STEAK, BRUSH IT WITH BUTTER AND TOSS ON THE BROILER FOR THE HOT, SEARING FLAME TO BROWN RAPIDLY. ONE SIDE'S FINISHED AND OVER IT GOES FOR A SIZZLING ON T'OTHER SIDE. BEFORE THE BAKED IDAHO POTATO IS POPPED OPEN AND A CHUNK OF BUTTER INSERTED, THE STEAK'S FINISHED AND ALL IS SET BEFORE YOU. A RIVERSIDE FEATURE AT DINNER THESE WINTER NIGHTS.

EARLY BIRD DEPOSITS ARE COMING IN RAPIDLY. DID YOU SEND YOURS? BETTER PLAY IT SAFE THIS YEAR – YOU CAN'T LOSE WITH A RESERVATION DEPOSIT NOW. AND YOU DO HAVE PRIORITY!

JUST AHEAD – ST. PATRICK'S DAY, MARCH 17TH; PALM SUNDAY, MARCH 25TH; EASTER, APRIL 1ST. THESE DATES ARE SOON AT HAND. DON'T BE DISAPPOINTED, BETTER RESERVE NOW FOR THE CHOICEST ACCOMMODATIONS.

SHALL WE SEE YOU SOON?

CORDIALLY,

Frank Parke

Newsletter from February 1956.

RIVERSIDE NEWS

| DECEMBER – 1955 | THE RIVERSIDE INN – CAMBRIDGE SPRINGS, PA. | PHONE 2981 |

CHRISTMAS WAS THE FRIST HOLIDAY OR HOLY DAY AND OF COURSE WE CELEBRATE IT WITH GREAT REVERENCE AND JOY. THE HOLY FAMILY INSPIRES EACH OF US TO JOIN AGAIN WITH THE OTHERS IN OUR IMMEDIATE FAMILY AND IT IS A DAY OF GLADNESS AND MERRIMENT FOR CHILDREN OF EVERY AGE IN EVERY LAND.

IF ONE IS ALONE AT CHRISTMAS, HE OR SHE MIGHT WELL CONSIDER JOINING THE MERRY THRONG AT THE RIVERSIDE. YOU'LL FORGET ABOUT YOURSELF AND YOUR PROBLEMS AS YOU ENTER OUR DOOR. THERE'LL BE SOMETHING SCHEDULED FOR YOU FROM FRIDAY, DECEMBER 23RD., RIGHT UP UNTIL MONDAY, JANUARY 2ND. SO PLAN TO SPEND THE COMING HOLIDAYS AT THIS FRIENDLY COUNTRY INN – TREAT YOURSELF TO A MERRY CHRISTMAS.

BICYCLES ARE AT YOUR COMMAND THESE WINTER DAYS AT THE RIVERSIDE. INDOORS OF COURSE BUT YOU GET THE SAME EXERCISE AND THRILL AS THOUGH YOU WERE OUTDOORS IN BERMUDA.

THE TOBOGGAN SLIDE IS ABOUT READY. ENTRANCE IS JUST OUTSIDE THE FIREPLACE LOUNGE. THE 64 FEET OF WOODEN SNOWFILLED CHUTE DROPS FROM A PLATFORM ABOUT 25 FEET TO THE MEADOW BEYOND THE TERRACES AND YOU'LL ZOOM ACROSS THE "RUN" A FEW HUNDRED FEET TO THE PASTURE FENCE AREA. WE SHALL HAVE SEVERAL TOBOGGANS IN USE AND WE EXPECT THAT IT'LL BE A HEAP OF FUN. COME RIDE OR WATCH!

ICE SKATING TOO IS READY IN THE SAME AREA. A NICE SMOOTH 30 X 60 RINK WILL BE KEPT IN GOOD SKATING CONDITION FOR YOUR VISIT TO THE INN. ALL OF THESE WINTER SPORTS ARE OF COURSE DEPENDENT ON WEATHER CONDITIONS. AT THIS MOMENT THE WEATHER'S GREAT.

ARE YOU A SCRIMSHANDER? WE MEAN ONE WHO MAKES SCRIMSHAW. THIS IS A GENERAL TERM FOR SMALL, HAND CARVED ITEMS FORMERLY MADE FROM WHALES' TEETH OR WALRUS IVORY. A CENTURY AGO, AMERICAN SEAMEN ON WHALING VESSELS WHILED AWAY THEIR ODD MOMENTS FASHIONING OBJECTS RANGING FROM PIE CRUST WHEELS TO CRIBBAGE BOARDS. TODAY SCRIMSHAW MIGHT BE THE SMALL HAND CARVED FIGURES BEING MADE AND PROFITABLY SOLD BY RETIRED FOLKS.

POINSETTIA IS GENERALLY ACCEPTED AS THE CHRISTMAS FLOWER. USUALLY ALL RED BUT OCCAS-IONALLY WHITE, THIS BEAUTIFUL FLOWER WAS NAMED FOR AN 18TH. CENTURY GENTLEMAN OF SOUTH CAROLINA, JOEL R. POINSETT. DON'T KNOW WHY BUT PROBABLY BECAUSE HE DISCOVERED IT.

PLUM PUDDING IS PROBABLY THE BEST KNOWN OF MANY CHRISTMAS DELIGHTS. THIS TASTE TREAT CAN BE MADE AFTER MANY RECIPES BUT OURS IS DISTINCTLY ENGLISH. WE SERVE THIS DELICACY PIPING HOT IN NOT TOO LARGE A QUANTITY BUT AGLOW WITH THE AROMA OF FINE BRANDY AND DELICATE SPICES, THEN TOPPED WITH A GENEROUS MOUND OF SMOOTH, HARD SAUCE MELTING DOWN THE SIDES. WILL YOU HAVE OUR FAMOUS BLACK COFFEE SERVED WITH IT OR TAKE A DEMI-TASSE LATER AT THE FIREPLACE IN THE LOUNGE?

SHALL WE SEE YOU SOON?

WE'D LIKE TO WISH YOU ALL A VERY PERSONAL AND SINCERE

MERRY CHRISTMAS

AND

HAPPY NEW YEAR

AND ALL OF THE RIVERSIDE FAMILY

Newsletter from December 1955. (Front)
(Image courtesy of Elizabeth Parke Brown.)

WINTER ADVENTURES
AT A COUNTRY INN

SNOWY, WINTRY WEATHER IS FORECAST FROM NOW UNTIL ST. PATRICKS DAY IN MARCH.

SO, COME SPEND A BIT OF TIME AT THIS RURAL SPOT AND ENJOY THE SIMPLER THINGS

OF LIFE. WE HAVE TOBOGGANING, SKATING, NEARBY SKI TOW AND INDOORS THERE ARE

GAMES GALORE. TABLE BOWLING, TABLE TENNIS, SKITTLES, EXERCISE BICYCLES, HORSE

RACE, LABYRINTH, AND OTHER TABLE GAMES. TELEVISION AND LIBRARY, OF COURSE.

SLEEP INDUCING BEDS — DELICIOUS FARM-FRESH FOOD — ALWAYS AT YOUR COMMAND.

AT CHRISTMAS AND NEW YEARS

GIVE YOURSELF A PRESENT — SPEND THE HOLIDAYS AT A REAL COUNTRY INN —

THEN START THE NEW YEAR WITH RENEWED VIM AND VIGOR AFTER A HAPPY HOLIDAY.

THERE'S PLANNED ENTERTAINMENT DAILY FROM DEC. 23RD. UNTIL JAN. 2ND., A WIDE

VARIETY OF THINGS TO DO, OR YOU CAN BE LAZY AND SLEEP LATE. BREAKFAST 'TILL 11 A.M.

WRITE OR PHONE 2981 TODAY FOR RESERVATIONS — WE SHALL HAVE A NICE CROWD

RIVERSIDE, THE FRIENDLY COUNTRY INN AT NEARBY CAMBRIDGE SPRINGS, PA.

FROM
RIVERSIDE INN
CAMBRIDGE SPRINGS, PA.

SEC. 34.66 P.L. & R.
U.S. POSTAGE
P A I D
CAMBRIDGE SPRINGS, PA.
PERMIT NO. 24

FORM 3547 REQUESTED

MERRY CHRISTMAS

Newsletter from December 1955. (Back)

(Image courtesy of Elizabeth Parke Brown.)

CHAPTER 5

After 18 years of ownership, The Riverside Inn was sold in 1963 from Col. Parke and the Incas Co. to Royston Laboratories, Inc. of Blawnox and North Suburban Land Co. of Ross Township in Allegheny County. The purchase price estimated between $420,000 and $500,000. Joseph R. Royston Jr. was present for Royston Laboratories and Al Thompson for the North Suburban Land Co. Per the agreement, Col. Parke would continue to live at the French Creek Farm south of Cambridge Springs, and the Incas Company would also maintain a small apartment house and an office in the borough with the deal.

Royston Laboratories was an industrial coating firm, and North Suburban Land Company was a land development company for private housing and apartments. L.G. Royston remarked that the Riverside Inn felt like a good investment with new road construction, and that the location on Route 19, equidistant from Pittsburgh, Buffalo and Cleveland, would bring tourism and recreation to the area. They planned to add a 75 room motel, some boating

Welcome sign for Riverside's 1973 season. (Image from museum collection.)

and fishing facilities, a restaurant with seating for 200, and an additional 9 holes for golf. The new motel would also include conference rooms for both company's business meetings and conventions. They also planned on operating the Inn year-round.

Under the new owners, Charles C. Walsh became the new general manager for Riverside Inn. He had twenty-three years of experience managing Statler hotels and Stouffers restaurants all over the country. Under Walsh's new management the strict curfew of 11:00 p.m. with a "lights out" and "no noise policy" begun by Col. Parke ended. The *Pittsburgh Press* reported on September 13, 1964, "Mr. Walsh is carrying out a renovation program in the old 'Casino' designed to provide for meetings, conventions and social events. The second floor ballroom in this building, joined to the hotel by a covered walkway, has been air-conditioned. The first floor, heretofore housing bowling alleys and billiard tables, is being set up for meetings. Entirely new is a bar, built into a lounge that has been enlarged and provided with lobby and outside entrances. The dining room is to be air-conditioned. A new swimming pool has been built."

Alliance College leased Riverside Hotel for three years starting in September of 1966 to house male students during the school year. Their new dormitories were under construction up on the hill at the college. Riverside reverted back to being a hotel during the summer months. This arrangement delayed Riverside Hotel's opening date, normally April 15th, to after the first week of June. During this time from September to June, the owners planned on building a two story motel near the golf course. It never happened.

In 1972 Riverside Inn and Golf Course were sold to James R. Anderson, from Royston Laboratories Inc. and North Suburban Land Co. Anderson had been the former general manager at Cross Creek Resort in Titusville since 1967. He and his wife Jean were active in management and opened Riverside for the summer season in May. They were the fifth owners of the Inn.

Myron Brink bought the Golf Course in 1974 with the option to buy the Hotel for $50,000, however Brink went bankrupt in 1975.

James and Jean Anderson sold Riverside Inn to Norm Zimmer, Jack Walsh, Jim Skelton, Donna Wright, and Larry Hayes in 1975. These partners formed

This picture catches a rare view of the east side of the Casino in the years before the back porch was closed in for the dinner theater kitchen. Clearly visible is the steps to the now-neglected Riverside Park along the creek. (Image courtesy of Crawford County Planning Commission.)

By 1977 the Riverside barn to the north of the hotel was still holding its own. Structurally, the barn was in great shape though used for little more than storage. It wasn't until three main beams were removed by Jim Anderson for use at the golf course clubhouse that the barn began to suffer. In spite of the cables used to hold it together, winter snows in late January 1981 caused its collapse. An article from the February 4, 1981, Cambridge paper stated that plans were to demolish the back portion and repair the rest making a shorter barn. As warmer weather arrived, it wasn't long before it was clear that plans changed. The entire barn was demolished. (Image courtesy of Crawford County Planning Commission.)

Riverside Enterprises, Inc. When both the Inn and Riverside Golf Course underwent ownership changes for the 1975 season, the Riverside Golf Course was converted to a semi-private club causing the Riverside Inn to affiliate with a new 18-hole Canadian-American golf course, what is now the Venango Valley Golf Course four miles away. The resort at that time, usually operational seasonally, had not established a closing date. The new owners wanted to see how the resort did in the fall before announcing a closing date.

In 1978 head chef John Geronimo expanded Riverside's menus, adding a seafood buffet on Friday evenings featuring scalloped scampi, shrimp creole, stuffed whole trout, broiled mackerel with potatoes and vegetables. A complimentary appetizer with each buffet featured clams, oysters and jumbo shrimp. John Geronimo had been head chef at Riverside for nine years. He also planned to introduce an Italian buffet later in the season.

The National Register of Historic Places received Riverside Hotel's nomination form on June 30, 1978. The nomination stated that "Commercially the Riverside Hotel exemplifies the mineral water craze which swept the country during the late 19th and early 20th centuries. It was the first hotel built in the county designed to provide the full range of services necessary to 'Taking the cure'. Also the Riverside Hotel is an example of the health resort hotel, a popular cultural and social phenomenon known as the 'mineral springs resorts." The Riverside earned its acceptance to the National Registry on December 13, 1978, and received notification of its status on February 2, 1979.

Mineral water on the property began selling again commercially in 1979. It was bottled at the Saegertown Ginger Ale Company. The water was pumped from the original spring discovered by Dr. John H. Gray in 1859. The 28 oz. bottles sold for 75 cents at the hotel, Edinboro Beverage, and the Saegertown Ginger Ale Company. It took six months to get approval from the federal government who demanded that the well be safe from flooding. The field holding the well was located in the middle of French Creek's flood plain. The well head was elevated above high water and had to be properly packed at ground level so that it would not be contaminated from flooding. After that, the well head had to be inspected by the Pennsylvania Department of Environmental

Here is the front desk as photographed in 1977. This area changed little in its history. Woodwork was painted, and carpeting hid the tile floors. Other furniture is absent for an **unknown reason.** (Image courtesy of Crawford County Planning Commission.)

This is one of the bottles of sparkling mineral water from Cambridge Springs. The water was pumped from the original spring discovered by Dr. John H. Gray in 1859. Production began on June 13th, 1979, at the Saegertown Ginger Ale Company. The mineral water boasted 47 minerals and sold for 75 cents. (Image from museum collection.)

The fireplace shown in this image from 1977 captures the stately Second Empire mantel and the George Washington plaque. Dating to before 1909, George didn't survive the 2017 fire. Oddly the bulk of the fireplace did. At the time of publishing, only the fireplace remains standing even after the remainder of the site was cleared, leveled, and seeded.

(Image courtesy of Crawford County Planning Commission.)

An advertisement placed in the *Pittsburgh Press* in 1972 from new owners Jim and Jane Anderson. (From The *Pittsburgh Press*, Sun, June 11, 1972.)

Resources to make sure it wasn't damaging the environment which took two years. Lastly, the Pennsylvania Health Department processed water samples with a mineral analysis before they issued a permit. In Riverside's newsletter it stated that, "The sparkling mineral water is organically pure, anti-acid, and acts as a diuretic tonic". The mineral water was boasting forty-seven different minerals.

Norm Zimmer tried his best to keep the hotel solvent, but it was becoming increasingly difficult. He sold the period furniture to replace it with more modern, less expensive furnishings. He even brought boxing to the casino in the early 1980's.

Adding to the distress, the Riverside barn's slate-shingled roof collapsed under the weight of heavy winter snows in January 1981. Norm Zimmer, Riverside Inn's general manager at the time, blamed the previous owner James Anderson. Anderson cut out three main beams from the barn, re-purposing the wood to build a patio at the golf course. He had replaced the beams with steel cables, but they could not support the weight of the large wooden structure and the January snows. Zimmer had planned to salvage what he could and shorten the length of the barn. Once warm weather came, plans changed. The entire barn, only being used for storage, was taken down.

CHAPTER 6

In the fall of 1983, Will and Terry Leavell, natives of Oklahoma, became the Inn's new owners. With an appreciation for the hotel's historical value, they tackled the mammoth job of restorations with the help of their organization's members. This work included repairing the roof, tearing up carpeting in the lobby (which revealed the original marble tile flooring), cleaning the newfound marble tile, and stripping paint from the discovered marble baseboards. To enhance the lobby and create a 19th century look, framed wallpaper sections were used and a fireplace was constructed from marble slabs discovered in the hotel's basement. Wallpaper removed from the ceiling revealed hidden swirled artistry. An area across from the bar was redecorated with roses cut from wallpaper and became known as the Rose Room.

During 1984, the Leavell's carried out many events to celebrate the 100 years of Dr. Gray's mineral waters being prescribed. Among the events, they built a parade float that was on display at the hotel's 100th anniversary of Gray's mineral water analysis from 1884. (Image from museum collection.)

With the hotel already enrolled on the National Register of Historic Places, the Leavells strived to have the Inn retain the character, charm, and flavor of its past. The Inn's massive dining room was renamed the Concord Room. "Concord" means peace. Other renovations were completed in the Fireside Room (back lobby) and the Grand Room (formerly the Casino.) The breezeway was screened and renamed the Strawberry Patch. All bedrooms were decorated, each with a different color scheme. Updated bathroom facilities and built-in closets were added. They added an in-house museum of memorabilia they discovered in the nooks and crannies of the Inn. Townspeople contributed to the antiques on display including numerous items from Ed Ledrick.

They opened the Inn from April to October. An advertisement for an overnight stay showed that you could rent a TV for the night for $2.00 as there were no TVs in the rooms otherwise.

In 1984 the century of Dr. Gray's spring was observed, and several events throughout the summer marked the centennial. The celebrations began with a May 13th Mother's Day buffet. Next was a Father's Day barbecue, complete with horseshoe and shuffleboard tournaments. On June 20th an Antique Fashion Show and Luncheon was held. A 4th of July celebration included an outdoor barbecue and games for the whole family. The day concluded with a fireworks display. On August 12th and 13th an Arts & Crafts Fair was held. The final commemorative events were held over the third weekend of September. On Friday a seafood buffet was served. Entertainment included a comedy skit and chamber music. On Saturday a gourmet buffet was served in the dining room followed by a dance in the ballroom featuring the Cambridge Springs Community Orchestra. That weekend also featured a parade float made by the Riverside staff. On Sunday an afternoon program began at 2:00 p.m. with special guests including State Representative Tom Swift, Crawford County Commissioner David Glenn, and Janet Derrington, the daughter of Col. Francis Parke representing her father. A plaque dedication and boardwalk restoration briefing followed, and refreshments were served.

Plans for the boardwalk never materialized. Some controversy surrounded the new ownership, and after a short two-year run, the hotel would be sold again.

Model A car club at Riverside Inn from 1991. (Images courtesy of Victoria Hendrickson.)

In 1985 Mike and Marie Halliday bought the Riverside Hotel, which by then had seen its better days and a beginning of rebirth by the Leavells. The seventy-five room Inn took a lot of energy and resources to restore it to its former glory days. They started renovating room by room, maintaining the historical and architectural accuracy. Each room was decorated with antique furnishings, most all of which were bought at auctions by Mr. Halliday.

The dinner theater started in 1986 with a few weekend performances of "Fiddler on the Roof" in the ballroom. The idea for a permanent dinner theater came from someone who actively performed with the Erie Community Playhouse. He asked Marie if she would be interested in staging dinner theaters more often, and she said yes. He went on to perform regularly in the Victorian Room dinner theater.

The Inn's reputation for fine dining, access to the ballroom for weddings, reunions, meetings, and weekend stays soon spread in the tri-state area. Live entertainment at the dinner theater brought people into Cambridge by the bus loads and gave them an opportunity to step back into the Victorian era. The Inn's motto was, "We're just a few pleasant miles from everywhere!"

Riverside Inn continued to flourish through the 1990's and into the next century. By then thousands had enjoyed the theater, Mother's Day Buffet, and craft shows. Thanksgiving Dinner was very popular along with Blue Grass music festivals and other programs.

By 2007 the Hallidays, who were in their mid-seventies, were ready to turn the hotel and golf course over to someone else with an asking price of $4.5 million dollars. Mike had bought the Riverside Golf Course back in 2003 for $750,000, and it was part of the package deal. The Hallidays agreed to sell just the golf course in 2010 to Linda Christiansen and Patty Flood for an undisclosed amount.

In February of 2010 the Hallidays were able to sell the Inn to Brenda Evans and Ken Falkenhagen, both long time dinner theater employees of the Inn. A group of investors put up some of the front money and the Hallidays financed the balance of the money and held the mortgage.

For all intents and purpose, the historic Inn got off to a roaring start in 2010 with the new owners. Easter Buffet was served on April 4th, Spring Fever

The highway sign along Rt. 19 near the inn advertised the 2010 Fourth of July Celebration at the Riverside Inn. (Image from museum collection.)

2010 Celebration for Santa's arrival. Located in back lobby. (Image from museum collection.)

Music Festival brought crowds to listen and participate in the bluegrass-type music. A huge all day July 4th celebration was enjoyed by many and ended with a fireworks display. December saw a well-attended evening in the ballroom for Santa Claus's arrival. The year ended with a New Year's Eve celebration which had not happened for a long time. The Inn usually closed around Christmas Eve.

The Cambridge Springs Heritage Society presented a Mother/Daughter Victorian Tea Party and Fashion Show at the Inn on May 6, 2012. Models from town wore Victorian fashions from 1840-1890. Victorian era furniture from the Riverside Inn was on display. During the fashion show, tea and cookies were served.

During the fall of 2012, the hotel hosted a 100th anniversary honoring the beginning of Alliance College. Alliance alumni held weekend events that ran from October 5-7. A tailgate party, golf tournament, dinner-dance, and mass at St. Anthony's were all planned for the weekend.

Outward appearances of the hotel's activities and Dinner Theater seemed good in 2012, but by 2013 serious financial problems were coming to light. The Hallidays filed suit over default on the $1.8 million loan. State, federal, and property taxes had not been paid, and other financial problems were discovered. Ken Falkenhagen was no longer part of the group.

The summer of 2013 brought interesting notoriety to the Riverside Inn. The Travel Channel came to town to investigate paranormal activity at the Inn. The investigation findings aired in an hour-long episode entitled "Lethal Waters" which aired on the show *Dead Files*. The *Dead Files* team uncovered interesting historical research that they shared with the Heritage Society. As for the spirit activity, Heritage Society President Dale Docter commented in the society's 2014 newsletter that each would have to decide for themselves what they chose to believe or not.

In 2014 the Hallidays were once again the owners. With numerous obstacles to overcome, the Riverside Inn struggled to open on April 11, 2014. Many of the old staff members called and agreed to come back and work for the Hallidays and get the place up and running that year. Jeremy Ball, a former resident of Cambridge Springs and one time employee of the Inn, became the

Jeremy Ball started first season as manager at Riverside Inn in 2014.
(Image from museum collection.)

Manager Jeremy Ball checks in with guests at Riverside Inn. (Image courtesy of Meadville Tribune.)

manager for the Hallidays. By 2015 the Inn was getting the season started in April with the Riverside Music Festival. It was a warm weekend which lent itself to sitting outside, rocking on the porch, and listening to the music. Many weddings inside and out took place, class reunions were held, and the Inn was once again the place to be for all they had to offer.

Many events during the town's sesquicentennial celebration in 2016 took place at the Inn. In May the hotel hosted a tea and fashion show featuring 150 years of clothing. The event was a huge success with nearly 200 people in attendance. The event was co-hosted by the Heritage Society and included many local models. The Riverside Inn also hosted the Heritage Society's September program on the 130 year history of the Riverside Inn. In October a history night for the History of the Alliance College was also held in conjunction with the Alliance Alumni Reunion Weekend.

In January of 2017, the early brochure of the Riverside Inn was posted on Facebook, and it looked like a great year of events was going to take place. The first dinner theater production was to be *On Golden Pond* starting on July 1st. Spring arrived, and the Music Festival was held April 7-9. The rooms were booked solid, and people came from all over to enjoy the music. The next Sunday was Easter, and over 1,000 came for dinner and enjoyed the ambiance of the Inn. April 29th the Adult Prom was held in the Ball Room. Then, on May 2nd, a devastating fire brought an end to all events. Dawn's early light bore witness that one hundred and thirty years of history were now just cherished memories.

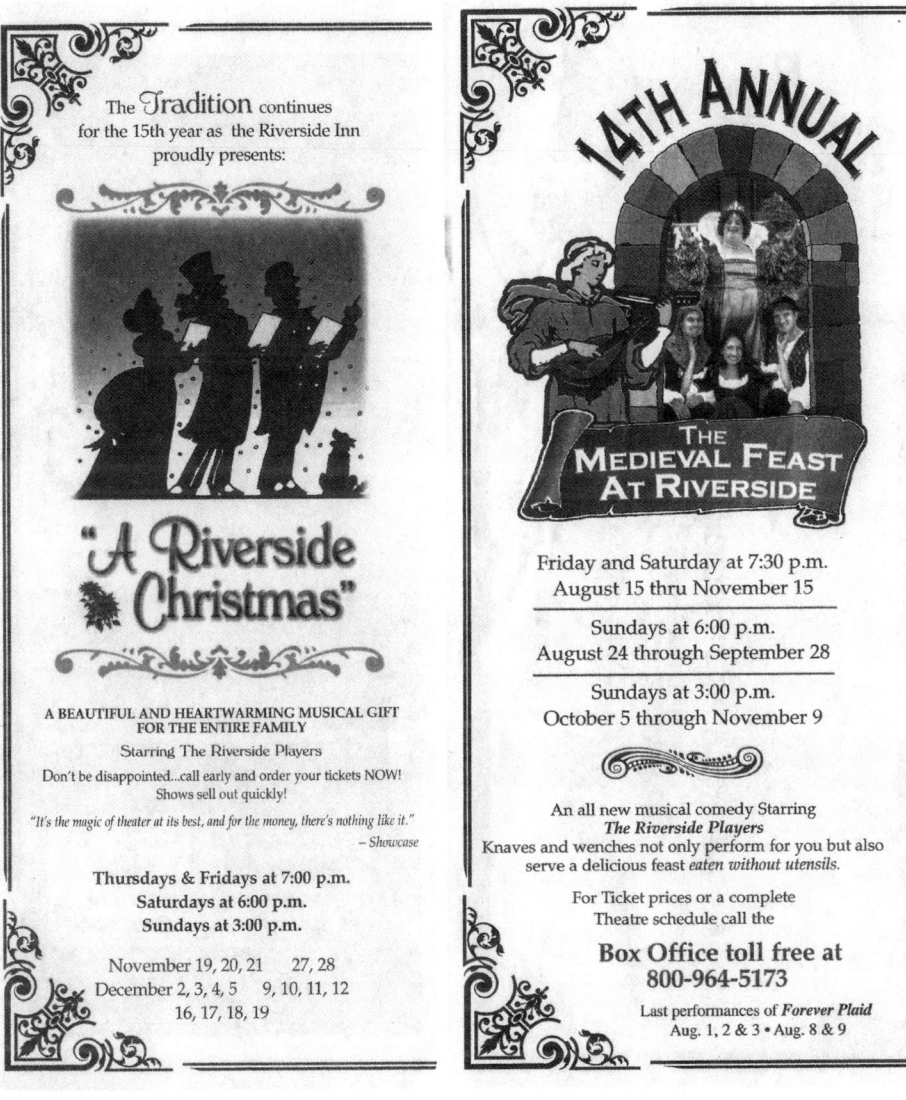

The Tradition continues
for the 15th year as the Riverside Inn
proudly presents:

"A Riverside Christmas"

A BEAUTIFUL AND HEARTWARMING MUSICAL GIFT
FOR THE ENTIRE FAMILY

Starring The Riverside Players

Don't be disappointed...call early and order your tickets NOW!
Shows sell out quickly!

"It's the magic of theater at its best, and for the money, there's nothing like it."
– Showcase

Thursdays & Fridays at 7:00 p.m.
Saturdays at 6:00 p.m.
Sundays at 3:00 p.m.

November 19, 20, 21   27, 28
December 2, 3, 4, 5   9, 10, 11, 12
16, 17, 18, 19

14TH ANNUAL

THE MEDIEVAL FEAST AT RIVERSIDE

Friday and Saturday at 7:30 p.m.
August 15 thru November 15

Sundays at 6:00 p.m.
August 24 through September 28

Sundays at 3:00 p.m.
October 5 through November 9

An all new musical comedy Starring
The Riverside Players
Knaves and wenches not only perform for you but also
serve a delicious feast *eaten without utensils.*

For Ticket prices or a complete
Theatre schedule call the

**Box Office toll free at
800-964-5173**

Last performances of *Forever Plaid*
Aug. 1, 2 & 3 • Aug. 8 & 9

The Christmas show, new every year, was a highlight of the holiday. The dinner theater show enjoyed a run from 1989 to 2016.
(Image from museum collection.)

Medieval Feast was another popular annual program in the dinner theater. It had begun as Canterbury Feast, but when director Paul Urbanowicz left to purchase the Station restaurant in Erie, the name at the Riverside changed to Medieval Feast. No silverware was used, only fingers, while dining on soup, salad, bread, stuffed cornish hen and dessert. (Image from museum collection.)

Riverside Inn

Concord Dining Room

Nestled in a beautiful, peaceful setting overlooking French Creek, the Inn provides the opportunity to get away from it all, easing the stress and grind of everyday life. The Inn is the perfect place.

...Just a few short miles from everywhere.

Soups & Starters

FRENCH ONION SOUP CUP 2.50 CROCK 3.50

SOUP DU JOUR CUP 1.95 BOWL 2.95

TOMATO BRUSCHETTA 4.95

CRAB STUFFED MUSHROOMS 6.95

SHRIMP COCKTAIL 7.50

ARTICHOKE FROMAGE 6.95

SALMON CROQUETTES 6.50

CHEESE PLATE 7.95

CRAB CAKE 6.95

The Riverside Inn

IS PROUD TO OFFER

HOUSE MADE BREAD, FRUIT BREAD, WHIPPED BUTTER, HONEY BUTTER AND A MIXED GREENS SALAD ALONG WITH YOUR CHOICE OF DRESSING AND SIDE STARCHES AS FOLLOWS: BAKED POTATO, WHIPPED SWEET POTATO, RICE PILAF, PASTA OR FRENCH FRIES.

DRESSINGS: HOUSE VINAIGRETTE, FRENCH, ITALIAN, RANCH, BLEU CHEESE, RASPBERRY VINAIGRETTE

CONSUMING RAW OR UNDERCOOKED MEATS, POULTRY, SEAFOOD, SHELLFISH OR EGGS MAY INCREASE YOUR RISK OF FOODBORNE ILLNESS.

Entrees

RED, WHITE AND BLEU NEW YORK STRIP
NEW YORK STRIP STEAK TOPPED WITH TOMATOES, ONION AND CRUMBLED BLEU CHEESE. 18.95

SLOW ROASTED PRIME RIB AU JUS MARKET PRICE

CAJUN SIRLOIN
10 OZ. TOP SIRLOIN BLACKENED AND TOPPED WITH ONIONS, PEPPERS, TOMATOES AND CHEESE. 14.95

FILET MIGNON
SIMPLY SEASONED AND GRILLED TO YOUR LIKING. 6OZ. 18.95 8OZ. 22.95

VEAL DA VINCI
HAND BREADED CUTLETS PAN-FRIED IN OLIVE OIL WITH FRESH HERBS AND MOZZARELLA CHEESE. 16.95

CHAR-BROILED CHOPS AUGUSTINE
BONELESS PORK CHOPS SERVED OVER COOKED WILTED GREENS WITH PINEAPPLE AND BLACK BEAN SALSA. 14.95

VEAL GONDOLA
CUTLETS OF VEAL SAUTÉED WITH MUSHROOMS AND TOMATOES THEN TOPPED WITH CRAB IMPERIAL. 18.95

PORK CHABLIS
BONE-IN PORK CHOP, PAN-SEARED WITH HOUSE SEASONINGS AND FINISHED WITH A CHABLIS BEURRE BLANC. 14.95

PASTA CAMBRIDGE
CHAR-BROILED CHICKEN WITH BROCCOLI FLORETS AND WHITE WINE GARLIC SAUCE SERVED OVER PASTA OR RICE PILAF. 13.95

BLACKBERRY CHICKEN CORDON BLEU
STUFFED WITH HAM, SWISS AND OUR OWN BLACKBERRY FILLING. 15.95

GRILLED CHICKEN
WITH HONEY, LEMON, THYME AND GREEN TEA REDUCTION. 13.95

CHICKEN FLORENTINE
TWO BONELESS BREASTS OF CHICKEN WITH BACON, SPINACH AND MUSHROOMS. 14.95

CRAB CAKES
SERVED WITH TRADITIONAL COCKTAIL AND TARTAR SAUCES. 15.95

CEDAR PLANK SALMON
A FARM-RAISED SALMON STEAK WITH CARMELIZED ONIONS AND BLACKBERRY COULIS, ON TOP OF, AND SERVED WITH A CEDAR BOARD! 15.95

SHRIMP PROVENCAL
LARGE SHRIMP SIMMERED IN TOMATO SAUCE WITH BASIL, OLIVES AND GARLIC. 16.95

MAHI MAHI
GRILLED AND SERVED OVER RICE PILAF WITH CITRUS RÉMOULADE. 14.95

2010 Concord Room Menu. (Images from museum collection.)

April 19, 20, 21! **NO CHARGE!** for admission

Riverside 2013 Music Festival

SPECIAL THANKS TO: **CAPLAN COMPANY**
CREEKSIDE GRILLE
MERCER COUNTY STATE BANK
WALKER'S BUTTONS AND BOWS * SERENITY INK
GRASSHOPPERS * JONES MACHINE AND ASSEMBLY
INTERGLASSTIC * LOCKE'S CUSTOM MEATS
AUTOMERICA INC. * FANE R. JONES *
THE BOOK TRADER * MIRROR IMAGE SALON
PATRICK PODPADEC

April 19, 20, 21!

FEATURING

Bernie Worrell
(Rock and Roll Hall of Fame Inductee
& Co-founding member of
Parliament-Funkadelic)
Hypnotic Clambake
Tiger Maple String Band
Adam Ezra Group
Blue Sky Mission Club

**Plus 38 other artists & bands
on three stages!**

**Including workshops,
demonstrations,
& music mall!**

Publicity card for 2013 Riverside Music Festival. (Image from museum collection.)

Riverside
THE INN AT CAMBRIDGE SPRINGS

2016 EVENT SCHEDULE

- Father's Day Buffet June 19, 2016 11AM-2PM
- Bobby Remp in Concord Dining Room June 24, July 29, August 26, & September 30, 2016
- Nelson Eddy Appreciation Society June 24-30, 2016
- Spirited Sleepover with Rogue Paranormal August 20, September 17, October 1&29, 2016
- Penny's Pin-Up Party September 2, 2016
- Chelsea House Orchestra in Concord September 9, 2016
- Alliance College Reunion October 7-9, 2016
- William Vrscak Workshop October 14-16, 2016
- Randy Riggle Show October 18, & November 19, 2016
- Halloween Party at Riverside October 29, 2016 9PM-1AM
- Thanksgiving Dinner November 24, 2016 11AM-6PM
- Christmas Craft Show November 26-27, 2016
- Breakfast with Santa December 3&10, 2016
- 3rd Annual Ugly Sweater Party December 17, 2016 9PM-1AM
- New Year's Eve at Riverside December 31, 2016

THE ELEGANT CONCORD DINING ROOM

NEW CHEF! NEW MENU!

Everything Freshly made IN HOUSE!

Buffets | Delicious Entrées | Daily Specials

2016 DINNER THEATRE SCHEDULE

- Lettice & Loveage
- The Fantasticks
- The Witch in 204
- Driving Miss Daisy
- 27th Annual Medieval Feast at Riverside!
- A Christmas Pudding
- Motel Mayhem: An In All Seriousness Production
- Visit theriversideinn.com for Prices, Performance Days and Showtimes!

LOUNGE AT RIVERSIDE

Sunday
Buy one appetizer; get one FREE with purchase of drink

$3 Sangrias 5pm-9pm

Monday
Movies & Manhattans

5$ Manhattans and popcorn

7pm-10pm

Tuesday
Trivia Night with Chef's Trivia Buffet

7pm-9pm

Wednesday
Wine Down

3$ Glass Wine, Cheese Plate Special

Thursday
Boneless Pecan Smoked Rib Tips

2$ Domestic Drafts

6pm-Sold Out

Friday & Saturday
Blue Diamond DJs 9pm-1am

Half Priced Apps 10pm-12am

Drink Specials

Room Reservations! Step Back into Victorian-style elegance in one of 75 beautifully decorated guest Rooms!

Since 1885

ONE FOUNTAIN AVE | CAMBRIDGE SPRINGS, PA 16403
THERIVERSIDEINN.COM | 814.398.4645

Stop by for a visit... We're just a few pleasant miles from everywhere...

2016 Riverside Inn schedule. (Image from museum collection.)

Front Lobby at Riverside Inn, 2016. (Image from museum collection.)

A view of the Ball Room, 2015. (Image courtesy of Lydia Todd.)

Porch at Riverside Inn, 2016. (Image from museum collection.)

Dining Room, view shows part of bay window, 2016. (Image from museum collection.)

Guest Room at Riverside Inn, 2016. (Image from museum collection.)

Guest Room at Riverside Inn, 2016. (Image from museum collection.)

George Washington plaque from pre-1909 above the back lobby fireplace. This was returned to its original location by the Hallidays. 2016 photo. (Image from museum collection.)

Breezeway, 2016. (Image from museum collection.)

A corner of the main dining room. (Image from museum collection.)

Fireside Room, 2015. (Image courtesy of Melissa Cornwell.)

Front view of Riverside Inn, 2015. (Image courtesy of Melissa Cornwell.)

A recent picture from L to R Marie Halliday, Jeremy Ball, Riverside manager from 2014-2017, and Mike Halliday. The Hallidays purchased the hotel in 1985, sold it conditionally in 2010, reclaimed the property in 2014, and were still owners again at the time of the 2017 fire. (Image courtesy of Jeremy Ball.)

LADY FINGERS

Used by Chef Robert Arter at Riverside Inn

32 dozen

36 eggs, separated

2 lbs. Sugar

1/2 lb. XXXX sugar

1 oz vanilla

2 lbs. bread flour

Method:

Beat whites of eggs. Add XXXX sugar gradually until stiff. Beat eggs yolks and vanilla until light, then mix with white of eggs lightly. Sift flour into batter and mix slowly. Fill pastry bag fitted with meringue tube and press on sheets of paper 41/2 inches long (Strips the size of fingers). Pour XXXX sugar in a small sieve and powder over lady fingers so they are coated lightly and evenly. Bake in warm oven 400°F for 8 to 10 minutes. When baked remove from paper.

Service:

Serve 5 to a portion a la carte. 3 to a portion table d'hote.

- American Menu Maker
Copyright 1936

CHAPTER 7

Monday, May 1, 2017, was a quiet day at the Inn after three busy weekends that had started the 2017 season. Janet Beanland from the local heritage society arrived at 10:00 a.m. to talk with Maggie Chmura, the front desk manager, and hotel manager Jeremy Ball about what the society could do to help with planning for the Riverside's Fourth of July celebration. As the conversation moved along, it was mentioned that the Red Apple Stitchers had already arrived Sunday from eastern Ohio and would be staying through Thursday. They particularly liked the hotel's Rose Room because they could stitch and leave their projects in the room until they returned for their next sewing session.

The day continued to be a quiet day. Jeremy left around 3:30 p.m. intending to go to the bank and then home to have dinner with his parents on McClellan Street. A violent rain, wind, and thunderstorm let loose about the same time as he was leaving. Due to the storm he scrapped going to the bank and went straight home.

Tricea Simcheck kept busy with her front desk duties into the evening. Bernadette Stefano, group sales manager at the hotel, was scheduled to come in at 9:30 p.m. and stay all night so the eleven ladies from the Red Apple Stitchers would not be left alone in the Inn. Bernadette arrived and helped Tricea finish up the paperwork of the day. Tricea left around 10:30 p.m. The bar was closed, the kitchen was closed, and C.J. Conroe, one of the chefs, came down the hall to inform Bernadette that he had cleaned everything in the kitchen, had run the usual checklist procedures in the kitchen, and was going home.

Bernadette was busy the next couple of hours working on the computer and keeping an eye on the front desk. Around 12:30 a.m., a couple of the stitchers came from the Rose Room, stopped to talk with Bernadette near the manager's office, and then proceeded to their room on the first floor at the north end of the dining room. Neither the heat nor air conditioning was on that evening, so all was especially quiet that night. At 12:40 a.m., there was no smell of smoke or of any indication that anything was wrong. Bernadette went back to her computer to continue working.

The in-house fire alarm went off at 1:00 a.m. As she didn't have the codes to enter into the system, Bernadette called Jeremy. Only having been installed in 2016, the alarm system would detect events involving fire, heat, smoke, water, or excessive cold and could have a code entered that in the event of a false alarm, the system could be overridden. If it were an actual event, then the alarm would continue. She entered the code, but the alarm continued. Jeremy instructed her to get everyone out of the building, and he would be right over. The system is wired such that if the code didn't shut off the alarm, then an automatic call would go to 911 and set off the fire whistle in town. The system did its job. The borough's fire alarm went off across town.

The ladies from upstairs were making their way to the lobby in their night clothes. Bernadette sent them out and went through the dining room to make certain the ladies at the north end were coming out. As the small group made their way back across the dining room, they heard loud popping noises and crackling from the kitchen. Smoke was coming around the door to the kitchen. Jeremy arrived and went through the dining room to approach the door to the kitchen, but the heat and smoke were too intense. The fire and police departments arrived on the scene in a matter of ten minutes. The worst-case scenario of any fire chief stood before him: The 130 year old Riverside Inn was on fire! All within twenty minutes, the fire had gone from an alarm to being through the front tower and spread to the back of the structure. Jeff Murdock, Cambridge Springs Fire Chief, directed thirty-one fire departments and over 200 firefighters to battle the inferno, but by morning the entire structure of the beloved Riverside Inn and Dinner Theater had burnt to the ground. It took two more days of putting out hot spots before the hotel surrendered to ruins and ashes. Since the fire had been so intense and devastating, fire marshals were unable to determine the exact cause of the blaze. One electrical engineer called to the site speculated that a lightning strike during Monday's severe storm may have hit one of the hotel's power lines. The surge could have run back into the circuits and festered there through the evening. The main panel boxes were in the rear of the kitchen, not where the cooking was

(Image courtesy of Jesse Cornwell.)

(Image courtesy of Jesse Cornwell.)

(Image courtesy of Jesse Cornwell.)

(Image courtesy of Jesse Cornwell.)

(Image courtesy of Jesse Cornwell.)

(Image courtesy of Jesse Cornwell.)

Aerial view of the ruins a day after the fire.

(Image courtesy of Meadville Tribune.)

done. This is where investigators felt the fire began.

Thankfully, the eleven ladies and three hotel employees in the building that night were able to escape unharmed. Bob Repa, one of the fire police, sustained leg and feet injuries while directing traffic when a vehicle drove over his feet. One bystander received a hip injury after a fall. Considering the three busy weekends the Riverside had experienced since their season had begun, if a fire was destined to happen, a really slow day in May was as good as could have been hoped.

A grieving community held a memorial service in the parking lot across from the ruined historic landmark on May 20. Some 200 townspeople, employees, and owners attended in an effort to begin healing from this tragic loss. In a bigger sense the fire consumed a building. When it is weighed against the enormous tragedies in the world, the loss of the Riverside seems minute. For those who have shared in its existence as employees, as attendees of the untold events held there, or as visitors seeking a quieter return to Victorian charm, the Riverside will forever be a part of all.

A memorial service was held in the parking lot on May 20th.
(Image courtesy of Jesse Cornwell.)

MEMORIES

We were the Red Apple Stitchers. A group of women from northeast Ohio who would travel over to the Riverside Inn for four days of embroidery, stitching, laughter, and making many, many memories. We have been going to the Riverside twice a year since 2007. It was always with great joy that we would meet with the staff, Bernadette, Donna, Candy, Sally, and others. Get caught up on happenings at the Riverside. Having spent so much time at the Inn we felt like part of the family. Retreat would begin Sunday morning, everyone gathering in the Rose Room as they arrived. It would take many trips hauling all of our stitching stuff into the room. Comfortable chairs, floor lights, table lights, charts, material, floss, extra items that we think we might need, and all our snacks for the table. Once in, we were settled. There would almost always be someone stitching in that room. From the first one up early before the kitchen opened till late at night when everyone else had gone to bed, even all through the night. You would also find stitchers on the porch. On those beautiful, and sometimes not so beautiful, days we would move chairs and tables into groups searching for good light.

We continue to hold our stitching retreats. We will never find someplace like the Riverside, and that may be a good thing. If we can't be at the Riverside, we should be someplace completely different. We would like to thank ALL of the staff for taking such good care of us over all the years. We will never find that anyplace else.

For eleven of us our last retreat at the Riverside began on Sunday, April 30, 2017. We were there on the morning of the fire. We were the last guests to stay at the Riverside Inn. Quite a distinction. After much discussion we have decided to change our name. We are now known as The Smokin' Needles.

- Donna Van Boxel
Red Apple Stitchers

Our adventure began in 1985 when Mike was told about the Riverside Inn. After seeing it, and with all its history, he loved it to the point that he bought it. After showing it to me, his comment was, "Don't worry, Marie. You only have to do the books!" My comment in return was, "But Mike, we don't know where to start. It needs so much!"

So we began with furnaces, air conditioners, kitchen equipment, tables and chairs. The list was endless. We decided we would add antique beds and dressers to achieve a Victorian look, knowing that it would take a long time to gather them.

Then we needed a staff to do the tremendous job ahead. I had a visit from Bob and Wilma Webster. Wilma was a gift from heaven! She was very bright, warm, friendly, and easy to talk to. She was hard working, accommodating, and could plan a party, a wedding, a dinner, or anything we needed. Along with Wilma came Maggie Chmura and Bernadette Stefano, two wonderful people for the Front Desk. Bernadette added the job of Group Sales, working with golf groups, business meetings, quilting and sewing groups, reunions, and art workshops.

Quite by accident, we added Dinner Theatre to our schedule. We started with John Wilkerson for a few years, and then Paul Urbanowicz came into the picture along with Rich Tryzbiak, Larry Evans, Charlie Corritore, Bob Martin, and a host of other talented people.

Among the other wonderful people, hard-working and loving the Inn, were Fran McCarthy, Ruth Woods, Donna Coburn, Heidi Morton, Patty Long, Donna Radwick Wermlinger, Sally Luce, Bob Potts, Carl Allen, Johnny Five (Tedesco), Brook Harrison, Hazel Webster, Barb Jacklett, Kathy Gosik, and Rose Smith. On the kitchen staff there were Cheryl Taylor, Bob Stewart, Norma Young, and Shirley Gromley, and in the Lounge, our very capable Bar Manager, Tammy (Burge) Wittmaak.

Jeremy Ball started in the dish room as a teenager, then went to bussing and serving, and in 2014 came back to be our General Manager. As Manager, he worked tirelessly these last three years to keep the Inn going.

Along with all of these, there was a host of part time people who were with us through the years.

We are so grateful for the many devoted people who, over the years, helped us to make the Inn a wonderful place where so many beautiful memories were created both for our guests and for all of us.

- Marie Halliday

I was, like countless others, devastated and heartbroken by the Riverside fire. Not only on a personal level, because I loved the Inn, but also for the huge economic and historic loss to our community. It was, for me anyways, one of life's "slap in the face/wake up calls," as to the fragile nature of life, and everyone and everything in it. How many of us allow ourselves to be trapped in situations that drain us of the time and energy to enjoy the people, places, and things that we hold dear? For days after the fire, I walked around "in a fog," praying to wake up from this nightmare. It wasn't until Saturday that I could bring myself to go there.

I was surprised even though 5 days had passed, that there was still a steady line of cars, almost bumper to bumper, driving past the Inn. It was a cold dismal, rainy morning, and it was creepy. The cars seemed to be like a funeral procession, which is how I felt... like I was there to pay my respects. I managed to find a spot to pull over. At that time, the parking lot was still roped off. I had a lump in my throat and a knot in my stomach as I stared in disbelief at the ruins. The smell of all the damp, charred wood was like the stench of death! Tears ran down my face the whole way home. I came in the house, sat down, and wrote the following Lament. When I was done, I felt, at least, a little better.

- Laura Carter

"ODE TO THE RIVERSIDE"

It wasn't just the beauty,
Of our Grand Victorian Lady,
It wasn't just that she held so much of our town's history,
safe within her arms.
It wasn't just the serenity
of her beautifully tended gardens,
her rambling porch,
or the babble of French creek out back.
It wasn't just her beautiful antiques and furnishings,
All lovingly restored and preserved.
It was a feeling.
A feeling that you were stepping Back in Time,
as you passed through her doors.
A feeling as though all of the energy,
from every event that took place in the last 132 years
was, somehow, still in the air.
And, it was personal,
To all of us whose weddings, anniversary celebration,
and other milestone events
that she so graciously hosted.
It was a feeling
which, I'm quite certain, I'll never experience again.
She was the heart of our town.
Our link to the past, and our hope for the future.
Only to be stolen from us by a cruel fiery thief in the night.
Such an undignified demise,
for such a Lady.
I only hope that somehow she knows
That no fire can ever steal our memories.
The Riverside Inn 1885-2017
May She Rest In Peace

- Laura Carter

It's a bittersweet memory to be married and celebrating at Riverside in 2015, and then being there again the night of the fire, watching the Riverside's legacy being burned to the ground. It was an eerily cold and quiet night, and I remember feeling the heat of the flames on my face. Our wedding was on one of the hottest days of summer. Tim, our photographer, captured a picture of our Chaplain, Sam, handing out handkerchiefs to the guys fully decked out in their tuxes in the Riverside's garden. I remember when Jesse and I first toured Riverside. We were blown away by its history, preservation and beauty. Riverside Inn was a special, and unique venue. Our wedding took place outside in the upper garden and reception was located in the ballroom. A string trio played under a white tent as people were seated. Many guests took advantage of the rocking chairs on the porch, where they sat and reminisced. After the service family and friends munched on homemade cookies and drank lemonade in the Breezeway. The Staff were wonderful. Jeremy Ball and Patty Glenn were with us every step of the way making sure the ceremony and reception went off without a flaw. I look back at our pictures now and think about that joyous time. Even though Riverside is gone, it will live on in our hearts.

- Melissa and Jesse Cornwell

A pervasive hushed silence enveloped the bystanders watching the flames and the many firemen bravely attempting to arrest the inevitable demise of our beloved Hotel Riverside. It was as though the sounds were turned to mute as the eerie spell continued through the night.

- Mike and Luana Bunting Moran

4th of July fireworks over the Riverside in 2010. (Image courtesy of Beverly Williams.)

On a picture perfect summer day, the inaugural July 4th celebration was held on the beautiful grounds of the historic Riverside Inn & Dinner Theater. The theme: "Step Back In Time for a Day of Family Fun & Fireworks!"

Events during the celebration involved demonstrations and activities by the 150th Bucktail Civil War Infantry and Historically Speaking with "Ben Franklin." On the veranda, displays included artifacts from the Civil and French & Indian Wars, the "Mineral Water Boom" by the Cambridge Springs Heritage Society, wood carving demonstration, Civil War Bucktail novels and antiques for sale. Also the veranda had tables set up providing dominoes, checkers, and cards. You could even learn how to play the Crokinole game manufactured here in Cambridge.

All ages entered the contests of watermelon seed spitting, pie eating and hot dog eating, complete with medals presented to the 1st, 2nd, and 3rd place winners.

Families enjoyed the refreshing pool as temperatures soared above 85 degrees. Many tested their skills at badminton, volleyball, croquet and corn-hole. Children were kept busy exploring the 1930's vintage fire truck, playing games, and having their faces painted.

Music filled the air with a live concert plus entertainment provided by the Dinner Theater's cast from *Ring of Fire* singing songs of Johnny Cash.

To satisfy appetites, the Riverside chefs and staff prepared a pig roast and BBQ plus other goodies to enjoy.

At the end of the day long celebration, thousands viewed the spectacular fireworks display over the historic Inn. The fireworks display was made possible by generous donations from businesses and individuals.

The safety of attendees was a cooperative effect between the Cambridge Springs Fire Department and the Police Department and CAVAS Ambulance was on standby.

The grand celebration was the combined efforts of the entire Riverside Inn staff and the community, truly making it another Riverside Memory!

- Beverly Williams
Special Events Coordinator

I've tried several times to compose some memories, but everytime my mind came up with endless memories and thoughts.

I first drove into the parking lot on a June evening in 1986. It was a dirt parking lot at that time, and the Inn itself needed much attention. Brandy, the Halliday's dog, was wandering around on the porch roof over the Dining Room.

I met with Mrs. Halliday for a few short minutes, and then she said to me, "Can you start tomorrow at 7:00 a.m.?" I replied, "There's a dog wandering around on your porch roof." She giggled a little and said workmen had been up there working, and Brandy must have crawled out on the roof with them and not come back in. She had someone from the wait staff go get Brandy.

Well, I did start the next morning at 7:00 a.m. I can't remember if I met Nancy Norman or Marge Drake first, but these two ladies "trained" me in the ways of the Riverside Inn. And we learned the ways of Mr. and Mrs. Halliday as we worked together. Shortly after I was hired, I actually got another job which I did take as it was full time, and the money was great. I talked it over with Mrs. Halliday, and she decided that I could work Thursday, Friday, and Saturday nights and Sunday morning. Those are the days that the Inn was open in the beginning. However, I worked those hours for many, many years to follow.

I can't really sum up on any one memory. The Inn was more than just a job, it became a home. I worked with some pretty amazing people. Everyday was different. You just never knew what was going to happen at any given time.

On top of the work memories, I also have family memories. The Inn became very dear to my family. My son worked as a waiter while he was a student at Baldwin-Wallace College. He would come home weekends and go back to school on Sunday after Brunch. My daughter worked in housekeeping for one summer. She always said that Mrs. Halliday "scared" her. We had many, many family gatherings at the Inn.

I always called Marie by Mrs. Halliday to younger staff and guests. She told me at the very beginning that Mike was to be called Mr. Halliday unless he told me otherwise. He never did, and to this day he is always Mr. Halliday to me.

- Maggie Chmura

May 15, 2016, I had been asked by the Heritage Society to be a model for their Fashion Show and Luncheon.

Cambridge Springs was celebrating their 150th Anniversary. That day it was snowing when we walked into the building. The Fashion Show and Luncheon was held in the Ball Room. I was really surprised when I came in. The room was filled up with lots of people sitting at round tables. Some of the ladies had fancy hats on, and the waitresses had long old fashioned dresses and bonnets on.

I got to model my Great Grandmother Beanland's Girl Scout uniform. It had been made by her mother, my Great, Great Grandmother Nora DeVore. After that I modeled my own Girl Scout uniform, so everyone could see how modern Girl Scouts look these days.

My other outfit was a girl's lacy white first communion dress that was from the collection of clothes from the Museum. I wore a pretty pink and white straw hat, long white stockings and white Mary Jane shoes. One of my favorite pictures is me in that outfit, standing in front of the fireplace in the back lobby of the Riverside. Today the fireplace is the only thing still standing after the fire on May 2, 2017.

Things I will always remember from that day: I made some new friends, my Great Aunt Janet Beanland was the Master of Ceremonies, my grandmother Patty Porter, and my step-mother Staci Porter were there to watch me be a first time fashion show model.

The summer of 2016 was very warm. My Great Aunt Janet would call the Riverside those hot afternoons, and if no one was using the pool, she would come and get me and my brother Wesley to go swimming. We would spend the afternoons playing in the pool and floating around on the inner tubes. Getting to swim in a nice pool with only three people in it was a lot of fun.

Little did I know, but the last time I would ever be at the Inn, my fifth grade teacher, Mrs. Henry, took our class to the Inn for lunch. It was before Christmas, because everything was decorated for the holidays. We had a class in Etiquette at school, so we went to Riverside to practice our manners at eating in a nice dining room. I can't remember what all we had for lunch, but I remember the soup and cake were very good.

After we had lunch, the class had a tour of Riverside and got to see all the pretty decorations. I am so glad our teacher had the class sit on the steps of the hotel lobby and get our picture taken. We were the last 5th grade class that got to go to the Riverside Inn for lunch.

- Paige Porter

Skyla Kebort and Paige Porter at the Tea and Fashion Show.
(Left image courtesy of Delores Hale. Right image courtesy of Janet Beanland.)

On May 15th, 2016, The Cambridge Springs Heritage Society and the Sesquicentennial Committee hosted a Tea and Fashion Show at The Riverside Inn in honor of Cambridge Springs's 150th anniversary. My four year old granddaughter Skyla modeled several vintage children's outfits for the occasion, including a cowgirl outfit, complete with hobby horse and matching boots, and a pretty blue dress.

It was a long and surprisingly cold May afternoon, lasting about 4 hours from dress rehearsal to the end of the Tea and lecture. My granddaughter was exhausted and hungry by the end the event. As we were leaving, she started to scream that there was a large spider on the porch outside, which was where we were headed. She absolutely refused to go out on the porch. We looked high and low, but were unable to locate any such spider. Finally we carried her to the car while she continued to sob. We had never seen her behave this way before or since about a spider.

Several days after the demise of the Riverside Inn, my granddaughter, now five years old, was visiting and we went to view the remains. I asked if she remembered modeling in the fashion show last year. She said that she remembered the pretty blue dress we borrowed from Rose Smith. Then she looked at me and said, "Grandma, I am so sorry about your Inn, but do you think that spider is dead now?" I couldn't help but laugh.

- Victoria Hendrickson

———————————————————————●———————————————————————

For over 130 years, the Riverside Inn has been the jewel of our mom's (Patricia Layton-Belfi) hometown of Cambridge Springs. Of our countless memories, our favorite is our grandmother's (Dorothy Layton-Fedorek) 80th birthday party attended by four generations of our extended family. We had never stayed an overnight however until this year when three generations of ladies visited for an amazing stay, capped off by an outstanding murder mystery dinner theater. Seeing my daughter (Erinn Diehl) fall under the spell of this magical place, where you felt like you stepped back in time when you walked through the doors, is an experience I will always cherish. So heartbreaking to lose this glorious place of history. Our hearts ache for Cambridge Springs - the Riverside was so much more than a hotel - it was the heart and soul of the tiny western Pennsylvania town.

- Stephanie Belfi-Diehl and Joseph Belfi

When I started at the Front Desk in 1988, I can still remember feeling how lucky I was that I got to come to work every day in those beautiful surroundings. After a few years, and moving from the Front Desk to Group Sales, I can also remember thinking that I couldn't see myself in any regular office or any other type of business after being there.

The sheer magnificence of the place, coupled with meeting all sorts of different hotel guests and working with nothing short of the best group of people you would ever want to meet, plus Marie Halliday as our boss made for the perfect job in my estimation.

Over the years, I never lost that sense of wonder every time I walked into the Lobby. I can still see it so vividly in my mind's eye even today. It is still difficult to accept that I'll never walk into that Lobby again. I'd like to close with the tribute that I wrote shortly after the fire:

"THE RIVERSIDE INN - THE END OF AN ERA"

We are grateful for the opportunity to have worked amidst her splendor,
For work that was so much more than just a job.
We are thankful for the many memories created, for guests who became friends
And for co-workers who became family.
She brought us together.
She brought us life, labor, laughter and love.
May She Rest in Peace, till we meet again.

- Bernadette Stefano

Everyone with The Nelson Eddy Appreciation Society (NEAS) was heartbroken when we learned that the Riverside Inn was completely destroyed in a fire on May 2, 2017. Our annual NEAS week long visit there was all planned for June 29, Nelson's 116th birthday.

Our group had been meeting at the Inn for nearly 30 years and the Riverside had become like a second home, a welcome retreat into the past in honor of Mr. Eddy, where we could surround ourselves with the true affection of the many employees who made our stays so memorable. Several of the staff have joined NEAS.

Marie Halliday ran a tight ship and everything was attended to by her and the staff. I remember once our group was going to have a "Hat Contest" luncheon in The Concord Room of the Inn. Marie felt it necessary to dress up our desserts by driving to town to purchase fresh strawberries just for our special luncheon.

Nelson Eddy was one of the greatest baritones of his time, and he is certainly not forgotten. The Inn was so ideal for our meetings, because it was a historic Victorian Inn decorated with turn of the century antiques. Each guest room was unique. I remember walking into the front lobby with its black and white tile floor, antique furnishings and pianos, a grand staircase where you would be welcomed by other members who arrived earlier. The entrance into the Concord Dining Room featured a lovely beveled glass picture window over looking the gardens and the wrap around porch that drew us out to the rocking chairs to visit or just take in the nostalgic glory. All during our stay, Nelson's voice greeted us since his music was played throughout the Inn.

We will never be able to replace those fond memories as no one could rival the service and commitment of the hotel and its staff.

Speaking of commitment, after the Inn burned down, Marie Halliday and Bernadette Stefano of the staff made arrangements at another venue so we could still have our annual gathering even though our scheduled date was less than two months away.

NEAS will never forget our many happy years at this grand old hotel. The Riverside Inn and Cambridge Springs, PA, will forever live in our hearts.

- Diane P. Flaherty
President - Nelson Eddy Appreciation Society

Whether you are a believer or not, the Riverside Inn ghost stories will at least pique your scary fancy! Just watch "Lethal Waters" from the *Dead Files* series, and you might just change your mind! Lots of ghost stories pervade the 130 year old inn's history. Tugs on a shirt, sudden chills in the air, furniture being pulled across the floor, objects disappearing out of the dinner theatre, sheets and blankets raised in mid air... and there's plenty more phantom fancy!

"Lethal Waters" set the stage, as a detective from Washington, D.C., is contracted to speak to the owners of the Riverside Inn and get the inside scoop on it's ghostly past! They were interviewed about their knowledge of events from both staff and visitor recollections. Their stories would later be correlated with a psychic medium, also contracted, to relay her experiences, after visiting each room in the inn. The medium knew nothing about the Inn, nor its ghostly history.

They began with the history at the original Riverside location, which was initially built as a sanitarium. It would eventually become a Mecca for those from near and far with health ailments. Years later eight thousand people per week would step off the trains in Cambridge Springs seeking healthy rejuvenation from the famed mineral spring discovered by Dr. John Gray.

As the Riverside owners articulated a history of ghostly happenings, staff and visitor sightings, deaths, and unexplained paranormal events, the detective carefully took down detailed notes. Next, the medium, who had been hired to spiritually tap into the inn's ghostly past, toured the entire Inn. As the psychic medium walked the many halls, she heard voices, saw images, and listened to messages she could spiritually "hear".

She saw a vision of a little girl, and a well-dressed older man with a handlebar mustache who appeared to be someone of authority. The medium then sketched the outline of this man, whose likeness was very similar to Dr. John Gray! Coincidence or not, there was an uncanny similarity to what details the owners relayed to the detective and the eerily similar interpretations of the psychic medium.

"Lethal Waters" hour-long presentation ends with a compilation of comparisons: the detectives notes and what the medium relates from her experiences as she "spiritually toured" the Riverside Inn. Her visions, spiritual communications, and details matched the notes the detective had recorded from the owners. She saw the origin of the Inn as a sanitarium for the sick, which she had no prior knowledge of. She relayed visualizing people drinking water, and in some cases being cured, while others succumbed despite the water therapy.

Staff and visitors of the Riverside Inn repeated seeing many similar apparitions like a woman in white seen by many walking along French Creek yards from the Inn conjuring people to enter the creek waters. Years later there were two reported drownings in the designated spots people had described seeing the lady in a white dress. How about the little girl playing in the halls and young boys arguing while being supervised to settle their spat by the older man with the mustache? Again, these visions matched the many recollections of former staff and visitors to the Inn and precisely described what the medium was seeing. Coincidence or fact?

More shocking were reports of what was going on in the Inn during the off-season when the Riverside was shut down. The owners would occasionally check out the building. They would hear the banging of pots and pans and sense that they were being watched. During these off-season months others reported seeing lights coming on and off during the night when no one had access to the building! Staff and visitors alike spoke of hearing footsteps behind them when there was no one there, or sightings that would appear as physical manifestations in period attire which would suddenly disappear! Many heard voices or saw shadowy figures in the halls.

Even more ironic are events that occurred the night of the fire which destroyed the 130 year old Inn early in May 2017. A group of twelve women quilters had worked late into the evening and had retired to bed just before the fire broke out. One of them reportedly complained of a pesky ghost making its presence known.

There were many pictures taken during the fire by locals on the scene. Some pictures appear to have apparitions in the windows and a woman in white standing just inside the front door of the Inn's main entrance. Photoshopped? No! As the fire raged a young high school student snapped some pictures which were specifically authenticated and turned over to the

Cambridge Springs Historical Society.

Not all staff or visitors of the Riverside Inn experienced these reported ghostly events, but there certainly appears to be enough spiritual interaction over the Inn's 130 year history to qualify such events as more than coincidental. There were visitors/guests who passed away at the Inn, those who were married there, had receptions in the ballroom, or those who had some other monumental experiences that touched their lives while visiting the Inn. Who are we to say they never spiritually left, that they, for what ever reason, could not part spiritual ways with this historical relic?

I grew up at the corner of North Main and McClellan Streets, so the Riverside Inn was a true neighbor. It's famous tower could be seen from my front porch. Many times we would hear the fire trucks and sirens come roaring over the bridge, turning onto Fountain Street. We would all hold our breath, praying that the inn would not succumb to a fire that would engulf and end it's historical legacy! If the ghosts of the Riverside Inn could speak to us, I am sure they would agree it will always remain a spiritual monument to the magnificent past of Cambridge Springs and as a haven for those who loved that beautiful old building with the white marble counter!

- Gay S. Hilton

I lived close to the Riverside, so when I was 14 years old I wanted to get a job there. I had to get my working papers and my social security card. I worked in the kitchen washing silverware and glasses, then I worked in the laundry area. And finally when I was 16, I worked clearing dishes from the dining room.

I also babysat a little girl whose mother worked as the Riverside office secretary. They lived in a small apartment in the Riverside.

My brother, Jack Newell, worked at the Riverside Golf Course and walked

Dorothy Newell and Donna Manross in 1949. (Image Courtesy of Viola Newell Powell.)

there every day. He had saved enough to buy a new bike, but the first day he rode it to work, it was stolen.

Our Mom, Dorothy Newell, worked as a waitress at the Riverside and walked back and forth to work daily, sometimes twice. At that time, her uniform had to be perfect: clean, starched, and ironed. She recalled that Col. Parke, who owned the Riverside, was a very strict employer.

My husband, Kenneth Powell, worked at the Riverside Bowling Alley downstairs putting the pins back in place. He later worked in the lobby helping guests with luggage as they arrived and left.

The Riverside was an important employer for young people. The opportunity to have a job was a big thing for us young people. For generations families from the area developed, and now treasure, their ties to the Riverside Inn and the Golf Course.

- Viola Newell Powell

Front row, left to right: Debbie Schmidt, Brenda Evans, Amanda Post
Back row, left to right: John Burton, Larry Evans, Paul Urbanowicz
(Image courtesy of Amanda Post.)

I have so many wonderful memories of spending time with family and friends at the Riverside Inn for Weddings, Bridal and Baby Showers, Birthday Parties, and Mother's Day Brunch, however, most of my time was spent with the Dinner Theater productions! I started with a production of *Hello, Dolly* in 1989, and was a cast member in countless other shows until the summer of 2013. That is when we brought *Always... Patsy Cline* to the stage.

When the Dinner Theater programs first got underway, they were held in the Ballroom. We would manage to change costumes and work around sets in the cramped back stage area, all while it looked effortless! After each show, when the guests had gone home or up to the rooms for the night, the cast would gather in the Breezeway. Each night owner Marie Halliday, would wheel a large cart in for us filled with food and drink, and we'd talk and laugh about all the little things that went wrong that night, and of course what went well! Marie would often sit right down with us and join in the fun. We would spend the rest of the evening in the Pub dancing the night away. In those early days, there were generally rooms to spare at the Inn. Cast members were given their own hotel room to put their belongings, get ready for the show, and stay the night. At the time I was finishing up my college courses at Edinboro University and would camp out at the Inn all weekend, using the quiet time during the day to study and get my homework done. The Riverside Inn always felt like a "home away from home" to me, and I appreciated the generosity and graciousness of Mike and Marie Halliday.

As interest and tickets sales increased, the large space under the Ballroom was then converted into the permanent Dinner Theater. I was a part of the annual Christmas show for years and also enjoyed attending productions with friends and family. *Nunsense* and the Medieval Feast were among my favorites. My most cherished memory is the year we brought *Always... Patsy Cline* to the Dinner Theater. My son Wyatt was eight years old, and it was the first time he got to see his mom "do her thing" portraying the iconic Patsy Cline to the delight of an enthusiastic full house. He had brought his 2nd grade teacher, who was also there, backstage... and he was So PROUD! Still to this day, when I'm involved with a big production, he likes to pick one performance and hang out backstage, talking with the crew, getting us water, and offering his thoughtful critiques!

The day the Riverside Inn burned, I joined former show castmates, friends, and community members in the parking lot... sharing tears and fond memories.

The Grand Lady will be missed, but never forgotten.

- Amanda Post
Nightly News Anchor - Erie News Now

I attended the original Nelson Eddy Elderhostel at Edinboro University when I was still much too young to qualify (about 42 years old) - so was passed off as someone's niece, if I remember correctly. I had simply been looking for Nelson Eddy sheet music and was referred to Perry and Lucy Pickering (of Baltimore, Maryland then co-presidents of the N.E.A.S.), who convinced me over the phone that I absolutely had to attend this once-in-a-lifetime musical event which would be taught by Edinboro University's English professor, Dr. John Marsh. The class was so well-received that first year, it was determined it would be repeated the following year, again as an Elderhostel.

However, by the third year the college naturally desired to vary its offerings, while those of us who had attended the first two years desired a continuation of the Nelson Eddy "musical course" with Dr. Marsh. I use the term "course" since in those early days Dr. Marsh would choose a theme and teach classes each day. He would compare Nelson's movies in various ways with other films and musicals of that era.

However, where would we meet now that we were no longer an Elderhostel group? Fortunately, Dr. Marsh recognized there was no better choice than the Riverside! As word spread through our quarterly N.E.A.S. Journal regarding the lovely Inn (offering a walk-back-into-time), Nelson fans began arriving from around the world, including from South Africa, New Zealand, England, Australia, and elsewhere, and of course from states all over the U.S. Attendees would oftentimes share personal stories of their experiences at Nelson's live performances during his concert tours. Over the years our "classes" eventually evolved into simply a desire among friends to merely experience Nelson's films on the big screen, along with others who esteemed not only his musicals but also his vast repertoire of concert music as well.

Our almost 30 years at the Riverside always included visits by guest baritones and well-known retired actors/singers, yearly member sing-alongs, visits to area points-of-interest, and annual talent shows produced by our own attendees. Although our numbers have indeed dwindled due to age and time, our memories from the beautiful and historic Riverside Inn and the many solid friendships which were formed will forever be etched in our minds as among life's most pleasant and enduring!

- Marilyn Held

A. Awesome – Amazing- Attraction – Alliance College Alumni

B. Beautiful – Breakfast with Santa

C. Classy – Christmas – Class Reunions

D. Delightful – Dinner Theaters

E. Exciting - Energetic – Easter – Employees

F. Family – Friends - Food – Functions

G. Grand Gardens – Guests, who returned year after year and became family – Guests from all over the World - Ghostly

H. Hospitality – Historic

I. Interesting

J. Jeremy - Jobs

K. Kindly

L. Lovely

M. Mr. and Mrs. Halliday – Memorable – Music – Mother's Day – Major Renovations

N. Nostalgic

O. Old – Organizations – Groups - Kiwanis

P. People – Pristine

Q. Quaint

R. Reliable – Relaxing

S. Sensational – Staff

T. Timeless – Thanksgiving

U. Unique

V. Victorian

W. Wonderful – Weddings – Work

X. Xmas

Y. Yesteryears – Youth

Z. Last letter and probable end to a grand hotel and many changes to our little community. We had so many fantastic employees over the years, and we all learned and loved sharing the beauty and history of the Inn. Many lifetime friendships have been made. WE ARE RIVERSIDE FAMILY!!!

Rest in Peace, our Grand Old Lady Riverside Inn

- Wilma Webster
Past Banquet coordinator

It shouldn't have been there.

It should have been a ghost, its remnants buried in pungent black soil and under sticky tan clay, kicked free by alert woods-walkers or revealed by the pings of patient metal detectors.

It should have lived on only in images on dog-eared post cards, in carvings on tarnished silver spoons, and in crumbling amber newspaper clippings.

It should have been remembered only by those fortunate enough to have heard passed-down accounts of its heyday, when trains and carriages flooded a community once known mainly as a preferred point to cross a winding and unpredictable creek with crowds of people, their numbers unimaginable today, in search of cures for their ailments.

But there the Riverside Inn stood, perched proudly yet serenely on its park-like setting on the edge of town, when I moved to Cambridge Springs a century after the mineral springs boom it helped create was starting to wane. I treated it as a curiosity at first, trying to understand during my first visits how this old, gargantuan wooden structure was able to remain relevant.

I came to understand as the visits became more frequent. It was the elegance of sharing a meal with family in the large, charming and typically crowded Concord Dining Room. It was the peacefulness of sipping a drink while enjoying a summer evening breeze on the porch. It was the serenity of strolling the grounds, of sharing a laugh in the lounge, of singing along with the performers in the dinner theater, of dancing in the ballroom.

There were memories to be made in a place like this, and I would go on to make plenty. The breakfast with Santa where my young daughter, my niece and my nephews were awestruck by being in the presence of the "real" St. Nick in a setting more heartwarming than the most beloved holiday scene. The Halloween parties were so packed with costumed revelers that it was impossible not to make at least a few new friends. The high school prom gatherings, where we parents smiled through tears as our young ladies and gentlemen posed for photos around the fountains and flowers. The occasions when we would run into friends and neighbors at the inn and would chat about how lucky we were to have such a wondrous place in our little town.

Like most things we love, we tend to take them for granted. I think of that often these days, as I look to my right while driving north on Main Street and see a large, empty hole where the inn's stately front entrance once beckoned. I should have gone to more dinners. I should have taken in more dinner theater performances. I should have spent more time soaking in the atmosphere on that beloved porch.

But when I start to get too down, I remind myself again that the Riverside Inn stuck around a lot longer than it should have. No one ever deemed it outdated and tore it down, or turned it into apartments, or let it die of neglect. We were all lucky to have the old girl for as long as we did. And I'm grateful for the memories she has given me.

- Tim Hahn

The Riverside Inn has been the site of many birthday parties and class reunions. Enjoying the ambiance of the hotel, sitting on the porch, visiting, laughing, rocking a summer night away was all part of the events.

Cambridge Springs Class of 1958 held their 75th birthday party in the back lobby of the Inn. It was September 25, 2015, and there was no better place we wanted to be as we celebrated 75 years of being on this earth. Always good food and service added to our fun evening of remembering our past school years and getting caught up on our present lives.

The minutes of the evening read: will gather again at the Riverside in 2018 to celebrate our 60th class reunion. May 2, 2017, dashed our plans with the burning of the Riverside Inn, along with many other classes planning to be at the Inn for their celebrations.

- Janet Beanland
Class of 1958

I have been attempting to compose this short recap of my memories of working at the Riverside Inn for days now. I never thought I would have to recount my memories in a book about our beloved hotel that is now just a memory. The many fond memories would fill more than the space I was allotted, so I will highlight some of my favorites based on the two different periods of time that I worked there that I'm sure that will spark some memories from my co-workers:

1990-1997
- The smell of Spic and Span at the end of a long night in the dish room.
- Always having full hands in and out of the kitchen, don't ever waste trips.
- Working The Feast on the dimly lit side porches of The Ballroom, especially the night I slipped and dropped a whole sheet cake pan of chickens.
- 'Funky Cold Medina' blaring from The Lounge on a busy Saturday evening.
- Afternoons at the pool between long double and sometimes triple shifts.
- Exploring Help's Hall late at night after one of our break room hang out sessions.
- Knowing it had been a successful day when Mr. & Mrs. H were enjoying their late night beer in the office.

2014-2017
- Working very long days with a fantastic team that was truly a family.
- Sitting in my office, that was Mrs. Halliday's office, and thinking how amazing the place was and how the challenge was incredible.
- Surviving the most chaotic of days with a smile on our faces and continuing to provide warmth and hospitality to our guests.
- Watching The Inn get stronger and stronger and being a part of something bigger than one's self.
- The last crazy Music Festival where we just couldn't seem to keep enough beer in stock.
- The feeling of coziness when we were decorating for Christmas. The popcorn being strung by the front desk, and the housekeepers scurrying to get everything perfect.
- Relaxing on the porch after a long day's work and feeling proud.

The preceding is only a small reflection of what I will remember about the Inn. Thank you to all of our guests and our Riverside Family for even more memories. We are fortunate that our minds will be what keeps the memory of the Grand Lady alive. It was my first job and led me to continue my journey in the hospitality industry. For me, the road turned full circle, and once again I found myself at home again only a few miles from everywhere... And so it will remain just beyond the way, along the Ole Fountain Avenue of our memories.

- Jeremy J. Ball

The earliest memory I can remember about the Riverside Inn is in elementary school. We learned about using the proper silverware, eating soup the right way, using table manners, etc. After that we took a trip to the Riverside Inn to have a nice lunch. I had an amazing time of knowing the Riverside Inn throughout my generation and it will be missed, but it will be remembered in everyone's hearts... Thank you Riverside Inn!

- Nicole Burdick

Just a few lines in remembrance - I worked the front desk for three years and made such good friends. I moved on to the Dinner Theater for the next four years. I worked with Paul Urbanowicz who was the director and owned the name "The Canterbury Feast." No one else can use it. He took the name with him when he bought the Station, a railroad themed restaurant on Peach St. in Erie. There was lots of stuff in between there and here. I enjoyed it all.

- Sondra Fitch

The entire Alliance College family mourned the tragic loss of The Riverside Inn. The Riverside Inn held a special place in the history of the college and hearts of the alumni. The Riverside Inn was truly one of the last vestiges of Alliance College. During the 1960s the Riverside Inn was used as an Alliance College dormitory.

The Riverside's one time housing of Alliance students is ironic considering the college's connection to one of the other long lost grand hotels in the Spa – the Rider Hotel. At the time of the Rider fire in 1931, that landmark was the home of Alliance College.

During the time period of 1966 through 1970, the Riverside Inn served as a dormitory for Alliance College. The college had experienced an increase of enrollment nearly doubling in size to 630 students. Due to a shortage of housing, the college entered into an agreement with the Riverside to utilize the hotel as a dormitory.

The arrangement was a great fit, as the Riverside was usually closed during the winter season. After two new dorms were constructed on campus,

Former Kujawiaki in Riverside Lobby. (Image courtesy of David Matejczyk.)

Alliance College students being housed in the Riverside returned to campus housing.

The connection of the Riverside and Alliance College however would continue.

Through the decades, the Riverside Inn hosted many Alliance alum weddings, alumni board meetings, and reunions. Starting in 2001, the Riverside Inn began hosting the Alliance College three day long weekend reunions every two years. Alums of the college were delighted to return to what was once one of the college's dorms. Some former students would even ask to book their specific old dorm room for the events.

The college's 2016 reunion will always be etched in the minds of Alliance alumni given the loss of the Riverside Inn. The sadness of the Alliance College family was noted the day after the fire by Alliance Alumni President Mike Anderson: "By all historical accounts, when the Rider Hotel (then Alliance College) burned down in 1931, the Community of Cambridge Springs was heartbroken, and together with the Alliance family mourned our loss. With the loss of the Riverside Inn, we mourn together again."

- David Matejczyk

Dr. Blair Matejczyk receiving award. (Image courtesy of David Matejczyk.)

August 5, 2001, my sister and her husband, Roa and Norma Jones, were honored with a surprise party at the Riverside Inn for their 50th Wedding Anniversary. Their three daughters and families planned the event. The party was held in the Ball Room. Some of the bridal party and many friends and family enjoyed the food and ambiance of the Inn. The afternoon was spent remembering their wedding of August 30, 1951, held at the First Baptist Church of Cambridge and the past 50 years of their lives. Holding special parties at the Riverside will always be fondly remembered.

- Nancy Gage

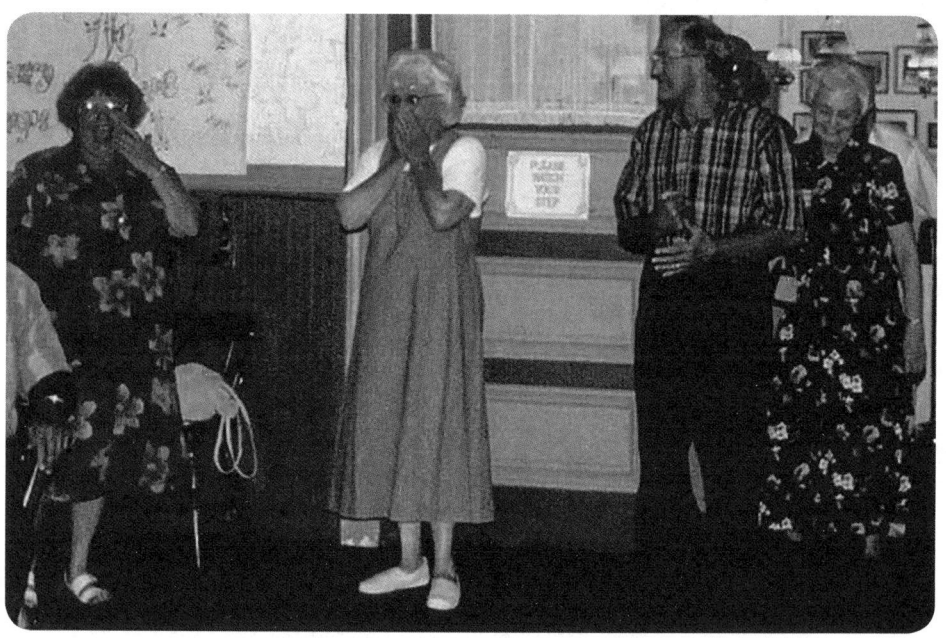

Being surprised in the Ball Room: Left to right: Janet Beanland, Norma and Roa Jones, Mary Beth Mead Decker. (Image courtesy of Janet Beanland.)